God is a Consuming Fire

Mark Burke

CONTENTS

Introduction

The Bible speaks a lot about the idea of fire. I am not a fire expert by any means. I know some basic things about what fire can do. It has a destructive quality in that it can burn trees, houses, clothes, and anything that is in its path. Depending on the way it is used in the Scripture, the word has different meanings. The Lord has been speaking to me lately about how He is going to be releasing His all-consuming fire in conjunction with His jealousy for the sole purposes of bringing purification, refinement, and function into the lives of individuals, churches, leaders, and nations across the world. I am feeling in the spirit this is a timeframe we are currently living in at this point.

It is not my intention to write another book on the fire or jealousy of God, because these resources have already been penned by our pastor and dear friend Pastor Ron Crawford.[1] Allow me to simply say, when God visits in His fire and jealousy, it is intended for the people of God to be purified and refined by the Spirit of Judgment and Burning and indicates a new thing God is doing in the heart and mind of the receiver. His divine jealousy must never be equated or compared to the human jealousy of mankind. Human and divine jealousy are not, and I repeat, not the same. God rises in this way because He passionately desires for all men to be functioning in His eternal plan and purpose He has predestined before the foundation of the world. We can do our utmost best to try and compare divine jealousy with things in the natural realm, but none of these really do it much justice. God is motivated with perfect desire and intent. On the other hand, humans, even those in partnership with heaven, must always realize we still have a carnal nature that is against the things of the Spirit.

---

[1] Please obtain a copy of the Fire of God by Pastor Ron Crawford from Pneumatikos Publishing at www.pneumatikos.com.

Close commune is necessary for us to continue to be renewed in our thinking and know His mind and heart. Let us turn our attention to several passages in scripture that speak of the all-consuming fire and jealousy of our God.

Chapter 1

Yahweh and Elohim: A Consuming Fire

Moses was a human being called by God to commune with God in remarkable ways. He was also one given powerful, revelatory things, too. The verses below speak of God being described as a consuming fire and a jealous God.

> ***Deuteronomy 4:23-24***   *²³ Take heed unto yourselves, lest ye forget the covenant of the LORD your God, which he made with you, and make you a graven image, or the likeness of any thing, which the LORD thy God hath forbidden thee. ²⁴ For the* **LORD [Yahweh-eternal plan] thy God [Elohim-heart of God] is a consuming fire**, *even a* **jealous God. [Elohim-heart of God]**

I love this because it speaks of some of the most remarkable facets of the person of God. I realize this is an Old Testament recounting, but it is still very much applicable in our day. There are many principles and realities which reveal and speak about God and His interactions with His people. We cannot, nor should we, put restraints on God. Can God really be restrained by a human being? Absolutely not. Who is really being affected in a negative way, anyway? It is the individual with the restraints. We are partners with God, and choose to move with Him, or not.

Take Heed to Yourselves

I think it is very interesting how the above verses begin. We need to remember that God is always relating to us on a very personal, customized basis. With Moses, He was telling him the importance of "taking heed," which is the Hebrew word **shamar.** It means to hedge about with thorns, guard, protect, or attend to. When this language is communicated, we need to make sure to pay close attention to the message. It is something very personal. God wants us to be a people that will protect and guard over the things He deems important and of priceless value. Why would He say these kinds of things to His people? For one, the enemy and his demonic forces are driven to bring destruction and division. They will do whatever is necessary to cause people to be led astray or forget the covenant of Yahweh, or His eternal plan.

Forget Not the Covenant

God continues telling Moses why this important for the people of God. He does not want us to forget, mislay or be oblivious of something. What is it that God does not want us to become forgetful of in this verse? The covenant that He has established with His people. His covenant for the people of God at the time of Moses was what God was establishing for the people at that timeframe. This spectacular exchange and discussion about the covenant is regarding the names of God known as Yahweh and Elohim. He is wanting to join with individuals, churches, leaders, and nations across the world in establishing His eternal covenant, which refers to His plan and heart. He is reaching out to make a new covenant with those willing to lay it all down to know Him.

Let me ask you a question. What is God covenanting with His people in our day? He is speaking freshly concerning what His plan and heart is doing in this hour. God is calling and inviting you to come into a phenomenal relationship beyond anything you have ever known. We were made to function as partners with Him on earth as it is in heaven.

No Idolatrous Practices

Equally important are the words of God for His people to not allow any idolatrous practices. The Scripture is very clear that these enticements will lead to destruction and dysfunction. He commands us to not partake of these kinds of things when He says they are forbidden. We must not give our passions to these kinds of devices. Everyone or anything can become an idol. It takes on many different forms in the physical and could be in our hearts. God wants us to give Him our whole being. This leads me to the incredible realness of the plan and jealousy of God.

Jealousy of God

Divine jealousy is always focused on the people of God functioning and fulfilling the will of God. It has nothing to do with Him being jealous in the way humans refer to jealousy. He wants His people to be passionately pursuing what His plan and heart is desirous of accomplishing on earth as it is in heaven.

> *Deuteronomy 4:24   [24] For the LORD [Yahweh-eternal plan] thy God [Elohim-heart of God] is a consuming fire, even a jealous God. [Elohim-heart of God]*

I can tell you from the spiritual experiences and encounters God has so graciously allowed me to participate with Him in that there is no competition or human jealousy element to anything that transpires at the Throne of God in heaven. All of heaven has a laser-like focus and passionately desires for mankind to know and function in the eternal plan of God. It is a privilege to know God's plan and live in His heart. May we all be consumed by His fire and jealousy to see individuals all over the world come to know His plan and purpose for their lives.

Yahweh and Elohim Will Go Before Us

Another passage of Scripture that speaks of the consuming fire is found in the Book of Deuteronomy. God is speaking to His people describing how His plan and heart will go before them to devour enemy opposition. This is a display of how the consuming fire can function in different ways.

> ***Deuteronomy 9:1-3*** *[1] Hear, O Israel: Thou art to pass over Jordan this day, to go in to possess nations greater and mightier than thyself, cities great and fenced up to heaven, [2] A people great and tall, the children of the **Anakims**, whom thou knowest, and of whom thou hast heard say, Who can stand before the children of **Anak**! [3] Understand therefore this day, that the **LORD [Yahweh] thy God [Elohim]** is he which goeth over before thee; as a **consuming fire** he shall destroy them, and he shall bring them down before thy face: so shalt thou drive them out, and destroy them quickly, as the LORD hath said unto thee.*

In the above passage, the people of God were faced with opposition that was much greater and mightier. The enemy was known as the children of Anakims, and they had a reputation of being giants towering above the people. In fact, the Scripture described them as great and tall in stature. By all physical standards, the Israelites had no chance to defeat or overcome the opposition on their own. The Bible goes on to mention a question about the children of Anak. The question was, who can stand before the children of Anak? The children of Anak were known as giants in the land (Numbers 13:33); hence, their description as being great and tall. The real battle is in the spirit realm, and we must never forget that God is for us, not against us. He wanted His people to understand, or to know, His plan and heart was with them no matter what they were up against in the natural realm.

Likewise, those functioning in the plan and heart of God today must know this powerful truth. Yahweh and Elohim are going before us to destroy, or bring to a point of desolation, and drive out enemy forces. Of course, all of this involves being accomplished in the timing of God. We cannot simply quote this verse and expect immediate results outside of His timing. We can use it as a point of encouragement or as a reminder of how God can and will move in His consuming fire for us in the present or future.

A Good Reminder: Not Because of Our Righteousness or Uprightness of Heart

Moses continued speaking to the people of God in reminding them how Yahweh and Elohim were the Ones doing this mighty work before their eyes. Our righteousness is as filthy rags. We need to always remember it is because of the plan and heart of God that enemy forces are cast out and not any righteous thing we can do. Yes, we are His partners, but God is doing the work through us.

Deuteronomy 9:4-6 *[4] Speak not thou in thine heart, after that the **LORD [Yahweh]** thy **God [Elohim]** hath cast them out from before thee, saying, For my righteousness the LORD hath brought me in to possess this land: but for the wickedness of these nations the LORD doth drive them out from before thee. [5] Not for thy* *righteousness, or for the uprightness of thine heart, dost thou go to possess their land: but for the wickedness of these nations the LORD thy God doth drive them out from before thee, and that he may perform the word which the LORD sware unto thy fathers, Abraham, Isaac, and Jacob. [6] Understand therefore, that the LORD thy God giveth thee not this good land to possess it for thy righteousness; for thou art a stiffnecked people.*

The consuming, destructive fire of God came in this scenario because of the wickedness of these nations, and Yahweh[2] drove them out before the people of God. To cast out in this verse is the Hebrew word ***hadap***, which means to push away or down. God is and will be working on behalf of the saints as we enter new terrain and nations to drive out enemy forces. We must never lose sight of "who" is responsible for performing these actions. It is only through God that these types of victories are won. I am not saying we are stiffnecked, but what I am saying is we do not need to forget that we fall short sometimes. We do make mistakes and sin by missing the mark of God. May we remember where we have been and press forward to move into the new.

God is a Consuming Fire

The author of the Book of Hebrews identifies God as being a consuming fire. Look with me at the passage below to find out more about this truth.

---

[2] Please obtain a copy of the book Yahweh by Mark Burke from Pneumatikos Publishing at www.pneumatikos.com or www.passionateforhispurpose.com.

***Hebrews 12:22-29** [22] But ye are come unto mount Sion, and unto the city of the living God, the heavenly Jerusalem, and to an innumerable company of angels, [23] To the general assembly and **church of the firstborn**, which are written in heaven, and to God the Judge of all, and to the spirits of just men made perfect, [24] And to Jesus the mediator of the new covenant, and to the blood of sprinkling, that speaketh better things than that of Abel. [25] See that ye refuse not him that speaketh. For if they escaped not who refused him that spake on earth, much more shall not we escape, if we turn away from him that speaketh from heaven: [26] Whose voice then shook the earth: but now he hath promised, saying, Yet once more I shake not the earth only, but also heaven. [27] And this word, Yet once more, signifieth the removing of those things that are **shaken**, as of things that are made, that those things which **cannot be shaken may remain**. [28] Wherefore we receiving a **kingdom which cannot be moved**, let us have **grace**, whereby we may **serve God** acceptably with **reverence** and **godly fear**: [29] For our **God is a consuming fire**.*

Notice with me how the Bible says God is a consuming fire, or **katanalisko**, meaning to utterly consume. The context of this entire passage is addressing the heavenly Jerusalem, or city of the living God. There are innumerable angelic representatives in this spiritual place, the general assembly, church of the firstborn, God the Judge of all, and spirits of just men made perfect. Jesus is spoken of as being present as the mediator of the new covenant; and the concept of the sprinkling of the blood is mentioned, which speaks of better things than that of Abel.

What is interesting about all of this is we are called to come into this heavenly place and function now. We are the church of the firstborn and do not need to refuse communications that speak from heaven. To turn away in this instance refers to turning away or back. We need to be those who will be willing to hear from heaven. We are being allowed to function in an eternal kingdom that cannot be moved, or is immovable. To operate in this, it is essential that we have grace, or **charis**, which causes us to be promoted or elevated.

Why do we need to have this grace? Is it saving grace? Saving grace begins our new spiritual journey and relationship with God. No, it is a point of elevation with the sole purpose of serving God. To serve God is to minister to Him in full agreement with what He is desirous of accomplishing, and we do this with reverence, or **aidos**, which is a term that means with the idea of downcast eyes, bashfulness, modesty, or awe, and godly fear. It is at this point when God is depicted as a consuming fire. We must be those that welcome His consuming fire.

Now that I have laid the ground work, in the next part of this writing I want to shift gears a bit and share with you an encounter that happened to me recently during a time of prayer at a seminar in Dallas, Texas. I felt like it was important for me to write about the fire and jealousy of God, because it relates to the spiritual experience with God that I had . I was completely surprised and did not know this was going to take place. I am so grateful for this life-changing encounter and pray it will minister to you as it did to me in a profound way. God put an eternal imprint in my spirit on how things operate in heaven and around His Throne that is so different than the way humans operate here on earth. All of heaven has perfect focus on enforcing the will of God on earth as it is in heaven, and they are looking for those who will partner with them in this manner.

God is moving in His fire in this hour and going forth in

His jealousy. He passionately desires for people, churches, leaders, and nations to be consumed with knowing and functioning in the eternal will and plan of God that is found in the heart and mind of God. It is the all-consuming fire of God for purification, restoration and function.

Chapter 2

Overwhelmed by the Lord

During morning prayer of the Saints and Angels seminar at The Father's Church in Dallas, Texas, I had an encounter at the Throne that was totally unexpected. I came into prayer with some words and phrases the Spirit was sharing with me regarding a passage of Scripture in the Book of Isaiah about fire and commissioning. As I entered a time of intercession, my spirit was active in a new way. I could feel the pulsing of divers languages and a shaking inside me. I knew God was speaking to me, but I was not prepared for what was about to happen. As this continued to intensify, I was overwhelmed in my spirit and fell to the floor. I felt the presence of the angelic in a profound way. I was reminded of the verse in the Book of Revelation of John being overwhelmed in the spirit and falling at the feet of Jesus as dead and the right hand being laid upon him, which speaks of the beginning of new partnership in working with the angelic.

Revelation 1:17-20 ¹⁷ *And when I saw him, **I fell at his feet as dead**. And he **laid his right hand upon me**, saying unto me, Fear not; I am the first and the last:* ¹⁷ *And when I saw him, I fell at his feet as dead.* ¹⁸ *I am he that liveth, and was dead; and, behold, I am alive for evermore, Amen; and have the keys of hell and of death.* ¹⁹ *Write the things which thou hast seen, and the things which are, and the things which shall be hereafter;* ²⁰ ***The mystery of the seven stars which thou sawest in my right hand**, and the seven golden candlesticks. **The seven stars are the angels of the seven churches**: and the* *seven candlesticks which thou sawest are the seven churches.*

As this was happening, I knew angelic representatives were very much around during this time of intense intercession. As I fell to the floor, I was carried away in the spirit. My spirit was continually declaring "holy, holy, holy" repeatedly. I knew I was before the Throne of God in heaven. While in this environment, I perceived things about this place that are so different than the way we as humans operate here on earth. Some of the things I was experiencing in the spirit are similar to the heavenly experiences that both Isaiah and John encountered, and I will do my very best to attempt to describe what transpired. I was completely riveted to the core of my being as all of this was happening.

I cannot begin to tell you how important it is for the people of God to realize their assignment and placement in God. The enemy and your carnal mind will try to tell you how insignificant your part really is in the Body of Christ, but he is the father of lies, not light. I truly believe God is wanting this kind of spiritual experience to be happening in individuals, churches, leaders, and nations across the world. One of the many insights in Isaiah 6 is found in Adonai revealing our placement and assignment in God. I became aware of this powerful insight, along with other revelations, that left an eternal impact on my mind and spirit. Paul wrote about the body being many members in one body and that each part is essential in order for proper function. Below is an extended passage of Scripture that bears many insights about the members of the body, as well as God choosing their placement and the importance of all the body parts are in His church. He has one body and wants men and women all across this globe to come into a divine realization of this fact.

1 Corinthians 12:12-26 *¹² For as the **body is one**, and hath **many members**, and all the members of that **one body**, being many, are **one body**: so also is*

*Christ. 13 For by one Spirit are we all baptized into one body, whether we be Jews or Gentiles, whether we be bond or free; and have been all made to drink into one Spirit. 14 For the body is not one member, but many. 15 If the **foot shall say, Because I am not the hand, I am not of the body**; is it therefore not of the body? 16 And if **the ear shall say, Because I am not the eye, I am not of the body**; is it therefore not of the body? 17 If the whole body were an **eye**, where were the **hearing**? If the whole were **hearing**, where were the **smelling**? 18 But now hath God set the members every one of them in the body, as it hath pleased him. 19 And if they were all one member, where were the body? 20 But now are they **many members**, yet but one body. 21 And the **eye** cannot say unto the **hand**, I have no need of thee: nor again the **head** to the **feet**, I have no need of you. 22 Nay, much more those members of the body, which seem to be more feeble, are necessary: 23 And those members of the body, which we think to be less honourable, upon these we bestow more abundant honour; and our uncomely parts have more abundant comeliness. 24 For our comely parts have no need: but God hath tempered the body together, having given more abundant honour to that part which lacked: 25 That there should be no schism in the body; but that the members should have the same care one for another. 26 And whether one member suffer, all the members suffer with it; or one member be honoured, all the members rejoice with it.*

Why am I saying all of this about the many members in the Body of Christ? It is crucial for the Body of Christ, those moving as anointed sons, to know their placement, assignments, callings, and giftings in God. Otherwise, there will be all kinds of demonic opposition trying to create schisms in the body in an attempt to divide and destroy what God is trying to accomplish. I know this is a current strategy of the enemy. The way to know your God-given placement and assignment is to seek the Lord; He will reveal this to each person who seeks hard after Him. Isaiah encountered this in his life, and God is highlighting this in our day, too. Open your heart and mind as we look at this together.

The Days of Uzziah Will Be Happening Again in Our Day

The day king Uzziah died, Isaiah had an incredible encounter before the Throne. Timing was a major part of this dynamic taking place. Everything in the kingdom of God revolves around relationship, authority, partnership, and timing. I believe these kinds of encounters are being released in this hour for those willing to humble and submit themselves to the process.

Isaiah 6:1 *¹ In the year that king Uzziah died...*

It is not my intention to focus on all the details in the account of Isaiah. I am only going to focus on certain aspects and what stood out to me. The timeframe in which the great prophet lived was very different from the day in which we are currently living. I am not prophesying death to any individual;, but I do know as it was in the days of Isaiah, these kinds of things will be occurring again. And as it happens, then men and women in the timing of God will begin to have these kinds of heavenly encounters. Uzziah died, and then Isaiah saw the Lord, or Adonai. Death will definitely occur, but maybe not in the way we think. These kinds of deaths will be determined only by God himself. Death has many forms and meanings. God will help His people to discern these kinds of things as we move forward together.

Seeing the Lord, Adonai – Placement and Assignment

After the death of King Uzziah, the Bible says something incredible happened in the life of Isaiah the Prophet. He saw the Lord.

> **Isaiah 6:1** *...I saw also the Lord [Adonai] sitting upon a throne, high and lifted up, and his train filled the temple.*

Let me pause for a moment of reflection about the spiritual encounter. As I was in the spirit, I knew and perceived the absolute necessity about all of heaven being focused on what they were doing as it relates to the eternal plan and will of the Father. It is so hard to put into human words this knowing and sensing I felt. It is so different than the way humans operate on earth from a carnal sense. We are so prone to allow other influences and our carnal nature to dictate what we say or do. Heaven is not this way at all.

During and after coming out of the intercessory time, I was flooded with all different kinds of insights and revelations from the Lord. One of these was about when Isaiah saw the Lord. The Hebrew word for Lord is Adonai, which really refers to the name of God that determines placement and assignment.[3] For me, I have read this passage many times, but not really considered the meaning of the word Lord. The experience and insight from God were astounding for me. My mind and spirit were welling up with such excitement and joy. I began to realize to a greater degree the importance of knowing our

---

[3] Please obtain a copy of The Name by Pastor Ron Crawford from Pneumatikos Publishing at www.pneumatikos.com

placement and assignment in God. Throne room encounters like this have purpose. God always has eternal plans and intentions for the things He allows us to experience in Him. We need to always remember this essential truth.

I know these types of spiritual encounters are going to be occurring in our day for various reasons. One is, the Lord, Adonai, wants individuals, churches, leaders, and nations to know their heavenly placement before the Throne of God in heaven. Second, He also wants us to know our assignments. God is fully capable of revealing these things to many people and locations across the globe at the same time. He does not have any limitations like we do, because He is God, and we are not Him. I am forever grateful for this truth.

Strategic Release of the Seraphim Will be Witnessed

The next sequence of things that transpires in Isaiah's spiritual place and environment is a strategic release of the seraphim was seen by the man of God, and his spiritual perceptions were activated in a variety of ways as he was having this amazing life-changing experience.

> **Isaiah 6:3-4** *³ And one cried unto another, and said, **Holy, holy, holy**, is the LORD of hosts:...*

In this spiritually-charged environment, one of these creatures begins crying out, not with tears, but as calling out to another angelic seraph declaring "holy" three times is the Lord of hosts. This is very interesting to me, because if you will recall in my recounting of the intercessory experience, I kept hearing the words holy, holy, holy coming out of my spirit as I was before the Throne in heaven. I remember this happening and came to realize I was joining in with the heavenly representatives in declaring the things that all of heaven are focused on around the Throne. A passage from the Book of Revelation was quickened to me as well, which speaks of the four beasts who are making these same declarations.

> ***Revelation 4:6-9*** *⁶ And before the throne there was a sea of glass like unto crystal: and in the midst of the throne, and **round about the throne, were four beasts** full of eyes before and behind. ⁷ And the first beast was like a lion, and the second beast like a calf, and the third beast had a face as a man, and the fourth beast was like a flying eagle. 8 And the **four beasts** had each of them six wings about him; and they were full of eyes within: and they rest not day and night, **saying, Holy, holy, holy, Lord God Almighty, which was, and is, and is to come**. 9 And when those beasts give glory and honour and thanks to him that sat on the throne, who liveth for ever and ever,*

The seraphims and four beasts in the Scripture are before the Throne declaring "holy, holy, holy" continually. It is a declaration for the restoration of the pure purpose of God to be known by people in the earth. This is what heaven is focused on all the time. I was in this incredible place and heavenly atmosphere God was allowing me to experience in Him, and I am forever grateful to Him for all that the eternal realm in heaven has impressed in my mind and spirit. When we pray and intercede before the Throne, God can and does open up our spiritual perceptions. I know in this hour He is calling His chosen ones into deeper dimensions of knowing His heart and His mind. I am learning so much right now about the way heaven is thinking and operating. Revelation is coming in different ways beyond anything I have encountered as an intercessor. I have known revelation and insight before, but it is at a much deeper level and coming because it is part of the timing of God for its release.

The angelic seraphs are making appeals for holy restoration, which is so important to recognize. They are also addressing and associating it with one of the names of God, the Lord of hosts, or the armies of the eternal plan of God. The holy is directly connected in this way to the plan of God with angelic hosts. I think this is a necessary insight into aspects of heaven that are remarkable. This revelation of the content of the angelic beings does not stop, though.

Seraphims Declaration in Heaven Around the Throne: The Whole Earth is Full of the Glory

Isaiah continues to speak and write about the very essence of the declaration of the seraphim while he is at the Throne in heaven.

> *Isaiah 6:3-4* ³ *...the whole earth is full of his glory.* ⁴ *And the posts of the door moved at the voice of him that cried, and the house was filled with smoke.*

I know I have mentioned this several times throughout this writing, but it bears repeating again. All of heaven, including the seraphims are totally focused on accomplishing the plan and will of God. They view and see things from a perfect framework and do not allow anything to prevent them from this mission. The precise, unhindered mode of operation is on point every time. They do not have iniquity or sin to deal with like we do as humans. They are declaring the way things should be in the earth, as God has determined this in advance. They see the whole earth from a global perspective; and according to their words, it is full of the glory. What an amazing view and perspective!

The encounter I had in heaven left these eternal

impressions in my mind and spirit. God made me aware of all of these things I am writing for you. I had known these kinds of exchanges and experiences in the past, but not quite like I am sharing with you now. Encounters like these are meant to cause lasting change in the life of the receiver. The objective of heaven is for the entire earth to be full of the glory. I believe God is about to manifest this in conjunction with the dispatching of angelic representatives to release holy, pure fire from the altar in heaven into the earth. When this begins to happen, it will signal a progression of voices, thunders, lightnings and earthquakes. The voices of intercessors will be ignited by this release to begin interceding and partnering with what is taking place around the Throne. Intercession is continually going on all the time. Jesus ever lives to make intercession for the saints to fulfill the will of God.

The Wilderness Temptation, Satan, and the Glory

The more I studied, reflected, and prayed about the spiritual encounter in heaven, the Spirit began to bring to the forefront of my mind how the enemy approached Jesus during the wilderness temptation. It is just interesting to see how Satan mentions the kingdoms of this world and the glory of them. Read this in the account of Matthew.

Matthew 4:8-11 [8] *Again, the devil taketh him up into an exceeding high mountain, and sheweth him all the kingdoms of the world, and the **glory** of them;* [9] *And saith unto him, All these things will I give thee, if thou wilt fall down and worship me.* [10] *Then saith Jesus unto him, Get thee hence, Satan: for it is written, Thou shalt worship the Lord thy God, and him only shalt thou serve.* [11] *Then the devil leaveth him, and, behold, angels came and ministered unto him.*

Satan has some knowledge of the glory because he mentions it in the verses above. He desires for sons to surrender in ***proskuneo*** to him in exchange for something else. Jesus Christ, the perfect Son of God, did not succumb to his devices. In this fallen state, the enemy recognizes deposits of the glory in the kingdoms of this world. His rebellion caused him and the other one-third angelic beings to be removed from the first estate, which means they are no longer in a perfected state. Iniquity was found in him, and this was his ultimate demise. We are not to bow down to any other gods, but to worship and serve belong to the Lord God alone.

I do want to reemphasize, that any encounter and its details are will only occur in the timing of God. After the death of a king, this sequence is set in motion. We need to remember this and know with absolute certainty God operates in this way. It is not something that can be fabricated or made to happen on our part. We can engage our spirits in intercessory prayer before the Throne, which will increase our possibilities of experiencing things like this;, but we cannot just make it happen. If it is ordained of God to happen, it will, in His perfect timing. I am only saying this because, like Paul wrote to the Corinthians, God chooses to temper the body as He sees fit. He alone determines when these kinds of spiritual things occur. As intercessors, we need to be content and feel a sense of fulfillment in our thoughts and spirit with where we are in Him and continue pressing forward into the depths of His heart and mind. All the parts of the body, whether external or internal, are crucial. Now, let us look at what happens next in this heavenly scenario.

Recognition of Personal Uncleanness During the Heavenly Encounter: Unclean Lips

As this dynamic encounter is happening to the man of God, he totally recognizes how unclean he is in light of seeing the Lord and the heavenly place and atmosphere he has been ushered into at the Throne.

> **Isaiah 6:5**   *⁵ Then said I, Woe is me! for **I am undone**; because **I am a man of unclean lips**,...*

I Am Undone

This is a very personal and close encounter that a real human being experienced before the Throne. I am purposely using human terminology, because I know some within the church would relegate this to a one-time experience just for Isaiah or put him on a pedestal as some superhero-like individual that God bestowed special privileges on. He was a prophet in the eyes of God, but he was still a flesh-and-blood person like us. We need to completely remove these kinds of thoughts from our thinking and truly believe God for life-changing experiences with Him. This was an encounter ordained by God, and not everyone is going to experience this. It happened because of his position and what he was going to be called to do on the earth. Your encounters will always relate to what God is asking you to do.

Living and being led by the Spirit is so vast and deep. The posts of the door were moved as this angelic declaration was being released, and the place was filled with smoke. What an experience that would forever impact the prophet we know as Isaiah!

These kinds of experiences are extremely humbling to the receiver. As I was in this heavenly place in intercession, I was totally overwhelmed by all the activities that were happening around me. There is no room for pride when these kinds of spiritual things are going on in and around us. God really does show you how magnificent He is, and you feel so unworthy to approach such a holy God. Everything about Him is perfect. All of heaven, which is massive beyond human comprehension, is perfect, too. Sometimes my finite mind cannot come up with words to describe what I encountered during the time I was before the Throne. I join with Isaiah and say, "I am undone."

After this journey in the spirit, I was totally dumbfounded or speechless. I did not have the words to even express what had just happened to me. I knew in my mind and spirit some things, but trying to initially formulate and translate it was very difficult. I immediately looked at how Isaiah responded and was like, That is it! I am speechless. I was feeling a sense of wanting to be silent and reserved before the Lord. After coming out of the time of intercession, I immediately got my laptop and began typing and putting things together in a Word document. I wanted to capture everything I could remember seeing, hearing, and sensing during the experience. It was overwhelming and precious all at the same time.

I Am a Man of Unclean Lips

Before writing the above heading, my mind just started thinking deeper about Isaiah's personal and verbal responses in being before the Throne. The essence of his declarations are so intriguing to me. Why did he feel the need to speak about his personal uncleanness of his lips? He could have said unclean heart or anything else. I believe it is because of his individual calling and gifting as a prophet, he came to realize in this heavenly experience before the Throne his lips were unclean. The Hebrew word for unclean denotes something that has been contaminated in some way. His lips were going to be used to speak as a prophet, and it was necessary for this to transpire the way it did for him.

When you are seeing the Lord, or *Adonai*, you come to realize a lot of new things about yourself on a personal level that need to be dealt with before being sent as an ambassador for the kingdom. I am not quick to judge, and neither should you be; but, it is much easier to be critical or judgmental when you are not in this type of heavenly scenario. When this starts to happen on a much broader scale in the church, leaders and people of all age groups are going to recognize they are undone and unclean. This is part of the experience no matter how much our flesh does not like it.

Recognition of Uncleanness in the People of the Land During the Heavenly Encounter: Unclean Lips

Not only did Isaiah become fully aware of his own personal uncleanness, he also came to the realization of how unclean the people were around him. Look at this verse with me.

Isaiah 6:5 ⁵ *...and I dwell in the midst of a people of unclean lips:...*

As we look at this verse together, I remind you of where this is taking place. It is at the Throne of God in heaven. The atmosphere and timing of this happening was ordered by the Lord *Adonai.* The revelation of his purpose and plan in conjunction with placement and assignment are the focal points. I think it is interesting that the progression started first with his personal uncleanness, and then he mentions how he dwells in the midst of a people with unclean lips. I am sure he could have focused on all the people in the land first, but this is not what happened. It can be tempting to get this in reverse order if we are not careful. God was wanting to do a work in the prophet, and he willingly submitted himself to this process of refinement of iniquity and sin. He serves as a great example for anyone in a heavenly encounter and process of how to respond when we are taken up to the Throne. Our uncleanness will be readily before us because we are encountering a holy and perfect place, along with God who is pure and holy.

Even as I am writing, my heart is consumed and my heart is overwhelmed by all of this. Just thinking about it causes me to sense how unclean and imperfect I am before Him. I do not mean this in a condemning way. I just stand in absolute awe and utter amazement at how God would want to even relate to us in such a deep, deep way. I know what was going through my mind during this similar encounter. My mind and spirit were overtaken and consumed by this experience as well as the feeling of absolute satisfaction and fulfillment. There is no greater place or activity that brings the same sense of satisfaction and fulfillment. It reminds me about partaking of eternal life now and not just when we get to heaven. It is on the mind and heart of God for His people to know Him in much deeper ways than they have experienced to this point. He is very capable of causing this to be ignited in you, but it does not just happen automatically. It might happen to you like it did with Isaiah, but it could also be very different and personal to you. Whatever the case may be, I can promise you it is an unbelievable, challenging, and mind-blowing experience. You might not use the words undone, but you will be totally speechless, like you do not have the words to express what just happened. Speechless in the sense of being completely stunned by it all. This kind of encounter will create submission and humility that is totally necessary in fulfilling the plan and purpose of God.

It seems like a painful process, but it really does not have to be unpleasant. Submission, humility and confession were the necessary components for the man of God. God can and will do His part when we, as His people, do what He requires. His requirements are motivated with complete purity and intention. He wants us to function and live the way in which He designed us in His eternal plan and purpose. He knows what is best for us. I am learning this continually through all the things I experience in this life and in the spirit. His heart's desire is for us to know and understand from His eternal perspective. This is one of the reasons why it is so important to continue in fellowship with Him by praying in the spirit in unknown tongues and the grace gift of divers tongues. He will grant revelatory understandings. With the Spirit's help, I am attempting to describe the spiritual setting and atmosphere a real human being encountered. It is truly hard and unfathomable sometimes to write about these things, because the human vocabulary and language seems inadequate. What happens next in this heavenly progression is a continuation of magnificence of our Heavenly Father in action with one He chose to fulfill with an amazing calling and assignment on behalf of the Throne of God.

My Eyes Have Seen the King, the Lord/Yahweh of Hosts

As this mighty encounter is unfolding, Isaiah continues to be so intensely impacted by the visitation that he proclaims, My eyes have seen the King, the Lord of hosts.

> **Isaiah 6:5** [5] *...for mine eyes have **seen the King**, the LORD of hosts.*

As I am reading the above verse, I am amazed by what is being referenced here. Not only did the prophet have a visionary encounter with **Adonai**, but now he mentions seeing the King, the Lord, or Yahweh, of hosts. Seeing the King in this manner involves the name **Yahweh**, or His plan, which is a reference to the angelic hosts. The names of God **Adonai** and **Yahweh** are verbally expressed by the prophet, which is very significant. This entire spiritual experience centered around his placement and assignment and the eternal plan which included angelic hosts. What a life-changing experience for this man and for us, too! We need to get this in our thoughts and never forget it.

God's placement and assignment and His eternal plan are so important for every person on this planet. The way to understand and know your purpose and placement is to become an intercessor. Hunger and thirst are essential. For me, I came to a point of desperation and wanted more of the Lord. I did not even know exactly what this would look like, but trusted God. This is when He opened the gift of divers tongues to me. It revolutionized my relationship with Him. It began this wonderful new journey in the Lord.

It is equally important for His church and the nations of this world to function in their appointed placement and assignments, too. From the eternal perspective, the Father has one church and one body with many members in it. I believe His Spirit is wanting to bring about a unifying work to the Body of Christ. When His Spirit invades the earth and the hearts of people, this unifying work will be readily known as a work accomplished by the Spirit of the Lord.

A Live Coal: Pure Fire Has a Purpose

The Bible continues by saying Isaiah encountered one of the seraphims flying towards him. This was all part of what was predetermined to happen in the life of the prophet. One thing is certain, it happened unexpectedly and was not on the spiritual radar of Isaiah. It involved his total submission and the timing of God.

Isaiah 6:6 *⁶ Then flew one of the seraphims unto me, having **a live coal** in his hand, which he had taken with the tongs from off the altar:*

Heaven is a real place, and we are invited to come up into this place now. We were made by God to commune with Him in this way. It is not only for Isaiah ,either. I think sometimes we forget he was a human being like us. Yet, God interacted with him in phenomenal ways, and He wants to do the same with us today. Of course, all of this is a part of the eternal plan and timeline of God for any person. Look with me at the verses below.

While Isaiah witnessed the angelic release, this happened for a reason. Seraphim means burning ones. They are fiery angelic representatives sent forth to accomplish the eternal will, objectives, and plans of God. Their appearance speaks for itself. They embody the burning fire of the place from which they have been dispatched in heaven. Hence, the reason they are called "burning ones." The actual root word for seraphim comes from **seraph**, which means to be set on fire. They are released with specific directives and purposes to accomplish. They are given orders at the Throne of God in heaven and dispatched at the direction of Almighty God.

It is very intriguing and fascinating to read this with you, because it speaks of so many heavenly realities. One involves the actual live coal itself. The other is how the messenger was to retrieve the red-hot coal by using tongs. I know God has an order and way of transacting things in heaven, and this representative followed His directives perfectly. As the seraph approached Isaiah, the Bible says the live coal was in his hand, or the open hand, which would represent a new beginning in partnering with God. As this happens, several things occur in the heavenly setting.

Live Coal on the Mouth and Lips

Perceptions and Giftings

First, the Bible says the burning hot coal is placed on the mouth of the prophet. In the past, I have experienced this type of burning sensation on my mouth several times over the years. It just happened suddenly where I felt like my mouth and lips were on fire. My first reaction is always to recognize what is taking place, followed by the Scripture of the angelic messenger touching my mouth. When this transpires, it is something that can be sensed and felt. Sometimes your carnal mind might tell you this is not real or it is a figment of your imagination. However, it is hard to ignore an experience like this, especially when it is personally manifesting in your body.

Just a word to those of you who are gifted as perceivers or feel things in the spirit. If you are not gifted as a seer, you can still feel the effects of an angelic representative laying this live coal on your mouth. If you do not see in the spirit with open vision, it is fine. Focus on using the capacities that are active in your walk with God. He will activate your spiritual perceptions to know when this is happening. Do not get upset or angry if your visual sense is not activated while this is occurring.

Dealing with Personal Iniquity and Sin

The next thing that happens answers the question, Why would God allow the seraph to lay the live coal on my mouth and lips anyway? The first purpose is to deal with personal iniquity, or twistedness. Second, it involves the burning fire to purge sin. God has specific purposes in mind when spiritual encounters like this happen in the life of the receiver. Look at the verse below with me, which speaks of this insightful visitation.

Isaiah 6:7 *⁷ And he laid it upon my **mouth**, and said, Lo, this hath touched thy **lips**; and **thine iniquity** is taken away, and **thy sin** purged.*

This is so interesting because the angelic being could have touched any part of the human body. He could have just as easily touched the head or forehead of the prophet; yet, God chose and directed to use an angelic messenger to do these tasks. From a human perspective, we can think of all kinds of ways God could have impacted Isaiah. God has specific reasons for all that He does even when we do not initially understand. I wonder what was going through Isaiah's mind as he is before the Throne witnessing and sensing all of these spiritual things transpiring. We know some of what he felt and even declared in the midst of the encounter.

The Bible gives specific details of what the angel was sent to do and accomplish. It is interesting what the messenger does with the live coal. The Scripture says he laid, or ***naga***, which simply means to reach and touch or to lay the hand upon. He was touched by a heavenly being on the mouth, or the place where he would declaratively be speaking the word of the Lord. As this happens, we know there must have been a burning sensation on the mouth of the prophet that was felt. This kind of pure, holy fire from the altar needed to be applied to the appropriate place where God would be speaking forth powerful words and messages through Isaiah. God is still desirous of this taking place upon the mouth of those called to speak on His behalf. Submission and humility are necessary for all of us, but particularly if you are called to be a prophetic voice to the people of God in this day.

After touching the mouth of the prophet, the seraph begins instructing Isaiah what the live coal has been sent to accomplish. It was not only for his mouth, but the messenger proclaims it needs to also touch, or ***naga***, his lips, too. In order to speak forth prophetically, the mouth and lips must have this live coal application. The seraph makes a declaration that it is to identify and deal with personal iniquity in Isaiah. Personal *avon*, means perversity. The root word of *avon* refers to crookedness or twistedness. This is why the messenger says, "thine iniquity." God wants us to allow Him to deal with our personal iniquitous tendencies. It must be applied to the declarative capacities in the mouth and our lips.

As I am writing this, a question comes to mind that I have not considered in this heavenly encounter. Why would God choose to use a seraph to lay the live coal upon the mouth and lips of Isaiah? It is a legitimate question that I have not thought much about until now. I mean, God could have done this without the addition of this spirit being, right? The answer is, of course, He could have conducted this on His own. One of the reasons is, God does things His way and not the way we think they should be done. The eternal mind and ways of God are so very different than the way we think and move. He directs and dictates the way these interactions are conducted because He knows best.

What does it really mean for the iniquity to be taken away? This is a legitimate question that bears being addressed because of the Hebrew term used in this verse, which is the word *cuwr*, and it refers to being turned off. Can iniquity be forever removed from us? Just a question I have been thinking about lately considering the purpose of the live coal. The Bible says the iniquity was "taken away," which is a word in the Hebrew that means to turn off. I do not believe iniquity can be completely removed from us. Jesus was bruised for our iniquities and His blood cleanses us from sin.

Isaiah 53:4-5 *⁴ Surely he hath borne our griefs, and carried our sorrows: yet we did esteem him stricken, smitten of God, and afflicted. 5 But he was wounded for our transgressions, he was **bruised for***

our iniquities*: the chastisement of our peace was upon him; and with his stripes we are healed.*

We are still flesh and blood and will continue to deal with iniquities and sin. Complete eradication of this will not come in this life, but only in eternity when we are with Him forever. If you turn something off, it means it could be turned back on at some point. I think of walking into a lighted room and turning off the light which causes total darkness. Or, walking into a room that is dark and flipping the switch, resulting in light filling the room. It seems to me that God is saying He has the capability with the live, red-hot coal from the altar in heaven to turn off twistedness from us for a timeframe. I am in no way saying we will not deal with iniquity. I am only saying God can and does allow for things to be turned off and on in whatever way He deems is fitting and necessary for us.

Jesus paid it all for our salvation by giving His life so that we could be forgiven from all of our transgressions, iniquities, and sin. But we still have the carnal nature, and part of this includes dealing with personal iniquities and sins. We are not perfect by any stretch of the imagination. The Apostle Paul continued to write about iniquity in the New Testament after the Cross, and James speaks of a "little member" known as the tongue that is spoken of as a world of iniquity.

James 3:5 *⁵ Even so the tongue is a **little member**, and boasteth great things. Behold, how great a matter a little fire kindleth!*

No Man Can Tame the Tongue

This is a humbling and sobering thought, to say the least. It almost seems like an impossibility, right? Well, it depends on our perspective and how we view this passage. James speaks of the tongue with great clarity and detail. Even though it is a tiny member of the body, it has the capability to have a major impact, depending on how we use it. I am bringing this to light because Isaiah had the live coal touch his mouth and lips, and I feel the tongue should also be addressed. The two parts previously mentioned are visible to the naked eye; however, the little member we use to speak or declare with can be seen, but does remain hidden. It is described as a fire with powerful capabilities which could cause a world of iniquity, or **adikia**.

This means our declarative member can have major points of impact. Hence, the word "world" being used here, which speak of the **kosmos**, or the orderly arrangement of things. Iniquity in the Old Testament refers to crookedness or twistedness. The Greek word **adikia** refers to the same concept; it just adds meaning to it by referring to injustice or wrongfulness, which really is a false showing and flows from twisted purpose.

What happens when we use our tongue, or declarative capacity that has fire, and speak forth in an iniquitous way? The Bible is very clear as to the negative ramifications of what is possible. Let's read this together and consider the impact the little member can have on the body.

> **James 3:6-12** ⁶ *And **the tongue is a fire**, a **world of iniquity**: so is the tongue among our members, that it **defileth the whole body**, and setteth on fire the course of nature; and it is set on fire of hell.*

As saints and sons, we need to be very cautious of how we use the declarative capability given to us by God. James is writing in a very direct way about how the body can be affected if we do not speak properly to the members. I know the context of this passage involves our communication and how we should be very aware of its capabilities. Once we all realize this truth, we will or should be less prone to speak anything that comes to our mind. I believe God wants us to be slow to speak, because He knows completely the damage that can be done with this little member He created to be used to declare His words. James says when it is used in a wrong manner, defilement to the whole body is the result. It is tragic, but so true.

The Greek word used for defileth in this verse is **spiloo**, and it comes from the root word **spilos**. Both of these terms combined mean to stain, soil, blemish, defect, and disgrace. It is a contaminant that we release into the body when we speak these kinds of iniquitous words. It can affect one or many members in the body. When James refers to the body, I believe the principle of the Body of Christ is applicable in this verse. Our tongue has incredible power either to bless or curse. The point is, we must not speak defiling words like these into the body, because it has extremely negative consequences. It is disgraceful, and we should be using words that speak and minister grace to one another. We will all make wrong declarations at some point because we our human; but when this happens, it needs to be personally confessed and cleansed quickly. Otherwise, the contamination can stain or soil the whole body. God help us all as we move forward in representing Him on earth.

All manner of beasts, birds, serpents, and things in the sea can be tamed by man, but the little member called the tongue is not able to be tamed by any man.

> ***James 3:7-8*** *[7] For every kind of beasts, and of birds, and of serpents, and of things in the sea, is tamed, and hath been tamed of mankind: [8] But **the tongue can no man tame**; it is an unruly evil, full of deadly poison.*

This topic is so important for all of us, not just individuals with prophetic giftings and offices in the church. We can all prophesy one by one. This is a word of caution for every member in the Body of Christ, or those functioning in a Christ-like manner. All kinds of animals, including those in the sea, have been tamed by mankind, yet the smallest member in our physical body cannot be subdued. Why is this the case? James gives us a few reasons why man cannot tame the tongue. One is because it is an unruly evil, which means it is an unrestrainable, *evil*, or *kakos*, or worthless. This is a perplexing concept, but it does reveal how our words can cause grave damage to those around us. This should really make all of us think very carefully before we speak. I know for me, as I am writing this, my thoughts and heart are gripped by what James is telling us. I am not trying to condemn anyone. I am saying we must be extremely mindful of what proceeds forth from our mouths. Pray in tongues and diversities of tongues. Unleash these kinds of languages in the spirit and pray for the understanding. All-consuming fire from the altar is what we need to be applied to our mouth, lips, and tongue.

A second reason why the tongue is not able to be tamed is because it is full of deadly poison. This puts what we speak forth in complete perspective. Our declarative capacity, or the tongue, has the capability of being full of, or replete with, death bearing poison. It has fatal and venomous qualities if not used properly in the Body of Christ. Poison is the potential for destroying life or causing harmful effects to the body. Our tongue must be brought under the control of the Spirit. We cannot afford to have caustic releases resulting in damage to the body.

Bless the Father and Curse Men

The reality of our tongue being used in an unruly and poisonous manner should provoke us to reconsider how we use our words. God speaks through James about realness of blessing the Father and cursing men.

> ***James 3:9-10*** *[9] Therewith **bless we God, even the Father***; *and therewith **curse we men**, which are made after the similitude of God.*

He is trying to get us to recognize we should not be blessing, or ***eulogeo***, or speaking the good word to the Father with our words and declarations, and then we releasing curses to mankind who is made after the similitude of God. Obviously, the people during this time were engaging as declarers of the good word of God and involved in words curses. The Greek word used to describe curses is ***kataraomai***, and it means to execrate or doom. To execrate speaks of a damning pronouncement of evil on someone or something. To bless or curse, that is the real question of which we should be forever mindful.

James continues by saying in the midst of releasing doom and evil pronouncement, we are actually cursing those who are made, or ***ginomai***, after the similitude, or resemblance of God. This is a dynamic insight into how damaging our speech and language can impact mankind who is made in the resemblance of God. It is not just enough to bless the Father, even though this is of utmost importance. As the people of God, we need to all take some time to reflect on how speak to God and other individuals who are made in His likeness. To be ***ginomai*** in His likeness refers to the way God has designed things to be for mankind.

What is the solution for this deadly dilemma? The Bible declares that blessing and cursing is proceeding out of the mouth of man, but "brethren" should not allow this to be the case. The analogy of a fountain, fig tree and vine are used to illustrate this point. A fountain does bring forth both sweet and bitter water, a fig tree does not produce olive berries nor does a vine bring forth figs. This is ludicrous to even consider, but it really does speak to the importance of what comes forth out of the mouth.

***James 3:10-12**   ¹⁰ Out of the same mouth proceedeth blessing and cursing. My brethren, these things ought not so to be. ¹¹ Doth a **fountain** send forth at the same place sweet water and bitter? ¹² Can the **fig tree**, my brethren, bear olive berries? either a vine, figs? so can no fountain both yield salt water and fresh.*

The question is, can a fountain bring forth both salt water and fresh? We all know this is an impossibility. The point is, even though blessing and cursing can come forth from the same mouth, we should not allow this to continue. Our mouth should be used for releasing and speaking forth the **eulogeo** to the Father and mankind who is identified as **ginomai** in the likeness of God. Focus on learning what is in your mouth before allowing it to come forth from your mouth. Identify if your speech will be focusing on the good word or if it will result in a curse. If it is the latter, do not speak. If it is spoken, quickly ask for the blood of Jesus to cleanse you and remove this from the record. This leads me to my next point of what God wants to take place when we focus on speaking into the lives of others.

I realize the passage in James says no man can tame the tongue. Let me ask you to consider a question. Can God, by His Spirit, help us in taming the tongue? He has the power to do anything for us. We all know this is possible only with the help of the Spirit. This does not mean we will function in absolute perfection with our words that come forth from our mouths. It does mean we can partner with the Spirit of God in helping us bridle our tongues. If you are functioning as a saint from your heavenly seat of authority, you must recognize how powerful His word is as you speak forth on His behalf. We are positioned at the right hand, the place where He releases the prophetic word about what He wants to do. Our placement in heaven is where we operate, we must continually submit our entire body, which includes the tongue, to be used in accordance with the way He designed it to function. Like David, we need the Spirit of the Lord, or Yahweh's plan speaking to us, and His word needs to be in our tongue. Our words need to be in alignment with the plan and purpose of God.

> *2 Samuel 23:1-3*   *¹ Now these be the last words of David. David the son of Jesse said, and the man who was raised up on high, the anointed of the God of Jacob, and the sweet psalmist of Israel, said, 2 The **Spirit of the LORD** spake by me, and **his word [the word of Yahweh] was in my tongue**. 3 The God of Israel said, the Rock of Israel spake to me, He that ruleth over men must be just, ruling in the fear of God.*

We just looked at how the tongue can be used for blessing or cursing. Now, I want to focus on another crucial insight regarding how we should be ministering to one another with our words. If the tongue is used properly in combination with relationship and the Spirit, it is potent in the kingdom of God and destructive to the enemy realm. We need to commit to using the tongue to release fire, blessing and grace to the hearers.

Proper Use of the Tongue to Release Fire and Blessing to the Whole Body

With this perspective in mind, Paul writes to the Ephesian saints and warriors explaining the importance of how we should be speaking to members in the Body of Christ. There is a connection here with what is coming forth from our mouths that is extremely important us to learn and live in expanding the kingdom. We need to be functioning in releasing the ***charis***, or grace, of God to those who are hearing what proceeds forth from the mouth.

Speak Grace to the Hearers

> ***Ephesians 4:27-9***   *[27] Neither give place to the devil. [28] Let him that stole steal no more: but rather let him labour, working with his hands the thing which is good, that he may have to give to him that needeth. [29] Let no corrupt communication proceed out of your mouth, but that which is **good** to the use of **edifying**, that it may **minister grace unto the hearers**.*

There are numerous insights in this passage of Scripture for us to learn valuable lessons. One, it is a message for those moving in an Ephesus-like walk and lifestyle in the spirit. The Ephesians were called to be saints and involved in spiritual warfare in heavenly places and much more. In our day, we are called to function as saints and warriors, and it is not coincidental that this writing is to people operating in these ways. The insight is here so we can recognize the power and authority God invested into these dear ones. Paul was prompted by the Spirit to write these words so people in the coming ages could become aware of the strategies of the devil and how to not to give place or foothold to any of his tactics. It is not my intention to focus on all the words and ideas in these verses. I do want to address the things I feel directed by the Spirit to highlight for all of us.

No Corrupt Logos Must Proceed from Our Mouth

As previously mentioned, our words and declarations are extremely powerful in the Lord. We are directed to not allow any corrupt ***logos*** to be released from our mouth. ***Logos*** is not corrupt from the perspective of God. Jesus is the ***logos,*** and it was with God in the beginning. A corrupt ***logos*** release speaks of a ***sapros***, or rotten or worthless, declaration of the foundational purpose of God. There is no corruption in the ***logos*** that was with God in the very beginning. It can become corrupt because of the way we perceive or receive. It has more to do with us, not God. He wants us to be in partnership with His foundational ***logos*** and communicating the purity of it. God is about releasing His Word, resulting in fruitfulness and value to those who are on the receiving end. This is so powerful for us to know, because the fresh insight will do a great work in our minds and our personal roles and responsibilities in the Body of Christ.

So, we just learned what we are not supposed to be doing. What are we directed to do or what next? Paul says we are to allow for ***logos*** communication to come forth in a productive manner, and this is referenced from the word ***agathos***, which is closely related to the ***agape***, or breathing hard after the purpose of the Lord. Out of an ***agape*** relationship is where we should be relying on what comes forth from the mouth. Our passionate love relationship is the source of our communication. In other words, from commune and fellowship with God, come words of purpose are spoken and exchanged. This is a two-way communication. We need to remember these powerful words as we move forward and continue to be those called to be ministers of the ***logos***.

When ***agathos*** is involved in this process, then the benefit is edification. We gain tremendous communication from Him and then use it to build up, not tear down. The enemy wants to destroy what God is architecturally designing by His Spirit. As the people of God, we must guard against the wiles of the enemy by standing firm. May God help us as we continue to hear from Him and then use what He gives to us to speak to the structural system of the body which results in construction, not destruction. He is building a spiritual house, and the parts of the house are very important. Edify the body with ***agathos*** communication.

The next question we need to address is, why focus on **agathos**, and using what comes from the active passionate relationship? This is necessary, because when the people of God operate in this manner with spoken communications, God's objective is to minister grace to the hearers. This is a principle in the midst of an Ephesus-like group that is essential in many ways. Grace is a part of one of the seven Spirits of God combined with supplication. Grace always brings an individual into a point of promotion or elevation in our relationship with God.

> **Ephesians 4:29** [29] *...that it may minister grace unto the hearers.*

In this light, we are directed to be ministers, which just means to give out something to those around us. Specifically, we minister or give grace, or focus on releasing things from our mouth that will cause promotion or elevation to those around us. This is critical for us to really see. God has designed this to be the proper way to release communications to one another. I just want to remind all of us of the capacity God has invested to trusted sons. We have been on this incredible journey for over fifteen years now, and our relationship with Him has yielded tremendous power and authority given to us by Him. We have to remember this and be very cautious not be give way to entertaining damning thoughts in our minds, much less release these into what God is building in the church.

You may have been wondering if I was ever going to get back to the Isaiah passage. I wanted to take some time to focus on the connection of iniquity and the tongue, because it speaks directly to the subject matter. Our words are very important, and the fire from the altar can deal with our iniquities, sins, mouth, lips, and tongues.

Now, let's get back to the Book of Isaiah to see what happens next in the sequence of events as it relates to the heavenly encounter.

Chapter 3

The Voice of Adonai: Placement and Assignment

Isaiah was allowed to experience things in the spirit when it was time for it happen. All the events in the Scripture, including being before the Throne, happened for a specific reason, and these only take place when God sets these in motion. It is all done in His timing.

Isaiah 6:8 *[8] Also I heard the **voice of the Lord**, **[Adonai]** saying, Whom shall I send, and who will go for us?...*

God reveals Himself through many different names in the Bible. Each one is very important. He could have chosen to speak to Isaiah in the way of His choosing. The Bible says he heard, or was ready to hear and obey, the voice of ***Adonai***. If we have learned anything up to this point, the voice of ***Adonai*** speaks of the placement and assignment for an individual. Adonai speaks very candidly to the man of God because He wants him to realize this, because it involves his individual assignment. As intercessors before the Throne, you need to know your assignments, because they are very important in this walk. The enemy will do and say whatever is necessary for you to not accept, know or fulfill the assignments God has for you.

Intercession is so necessary for this in our lives. Jesus is ever living to make intercession for the saints according to the will of God. He is at the right hand of the Father involved in this intercessory mode all the time, and it is the place where we are called to function in our intercession. Our assignments are those things our Father has called us to do before Him, and He never runs out of these tasks.

Think about this last sentence for a few minutes. Heavenly assignments never run out. Assignments are specific tasks given to us in our partnership. These are varied in scope and meaning for us individually. Only God has the capacity to assign all His people different tasks. He makes these determinations, and it is our choice to accept or reject them. The voice of **Adonai** is still speaking in our day, and is ready to give out assignments to those willing to come into partnership with Him. Isaiah's assignment came during this phenomenal encounter before the Throne. I believe this kind of spiritual experience will be happening for individuals and churches throughout the land.

Commission and Voice of *Adonai*:

Adonai begins to ask specific questions to the man of God. This is one of the ways communication is exchanged to us during these kinds of heavenly experiences. The godly representative starts by asking two clear questions to Isaiah that address his willingness to partner with God and with him being sent forth on assignment. The first question is, whom shall I send? The Hebrew word for send in this verse means to be sent out on a mission or assignment. At this point, the voice of Adonai was speaking to see if Isaiah would be willing to accept the assignment and mission at hand. The same is true for us; we need to be willing to move forward with whatever assignment is being given to us to accomplish. We have to decide to choose it. It will not be forced upon us.

The second is, who will go for us? I just realized a difference in what was spoken forth to Isaiah. On the surface, you might think these are just a restating of the same. They are not the same questions. The eyes of my understanding have been opened to see this difference. To go, or *yalak*, refers to walking. What does this mean for an intercessor who is partnering with God? It is not enough to accept the sending; it is equally crucial and important to partner with **Adonai** in walking out the mission or assignment being given.

Isaiah was commissioned and heard all of these things from the voice of Adonai. The assignments are endless, as God has much to do on the earth as it is in heaven. Divers intercession is so important, as it helps us partner with what God is saying and doing around the Throne. As we commit to continually coming before this heavenly place, **Adonai** speaks and commissions us to partner with specific assignments in asking us if we will go and walk out this entire process in the earth. What an amazing opportunity for those willing to hear from heaven and walk with God as partners!

Send Me

Being willing to accept the mission and committing yourself to walking it out in the earth, it is time to verbalize being sent forth to accomplish the task at hand. Isaiah willingly partnered with Adonai in this way.

> ***Isaiah 6:8-9***   *...Then said I, Here am I; **send me**.* [9] *And he [**Adonai**] said, Go, and tell this people,...*

While at the Throne in this encounter, Isaiah had some incredible visual, auditory and perceptive spiritual things happening. As the voice of **Adonai** continues to speak to him, he voluntarily accepts this mission and assignment not really knowing all the details. It is not just about having another heavenly encounter; it is about partnership with heaven to accomplish the eternal plan and purpose of God. As he commits to the task, Adonai releases more insight to him about what to do. This is the way He works in us, too. He wants us to be willing to accept the mission and the walk, and then releases more specifics based on our obedience.

Once Isaiah, or an individual hearing the voice and commission of Adonai, accepts this partnership, then words of going forth and speaking will follow. Adonai speaks by saying, Go and tell. The Spirit uses the same word previously mentioned when He says "go" or *yalak,* which denotes the walk or pathway. I think this is very interesting, because the person partnering with Adonai is required to walk the pathway laid out by the Lord. In conjunction with this, the same individual will be speaking forth words to those to whom he or she is sent.

One of the points I am making with all of this is we need to embrace both parts of this process. We need to willingly accept the pathway and to be declarers of what is being given to us to speak forth. We cannot just simply cherish being someone anointed by God to be a declarer of His Word. This is important; however, in this context when we are encountering heaven in this way and hearing the voice of Adonai, it begins with "go," or *yalak*, which means walking in the pathway that is before us without knowing all the details.

The Message from Adonai to Isaiah

Adonai continues speaking forth some really powerful words to Isaiah. On the surface, these words seem a bit odd or possibly even weird. To the human mind, or our carnal way of thinking, it definitely does seem this way. However, God knows exactly what He is doing even when we do not. His ways and thoughts are not ours.

Isaiah 6:9 ...*Hear ye indeed, but understand not;*

-Hear but not Understand

The first word spoken to Isaiah is for the people to hear, or **shama**,[4] which is a Hebrew word meaning to hear and obey. In this case, Adonai declares they will hear but not understand.

This sounds really bizarre for this kind of thing to happen, yet God chose to use an individual like Isaiah for this specific assignment and pathway. It was not going to be easy, but it would be priceless and full of fulfillment and meaning. To not understand meant the people were not going to be able to separate out things mentally that would cause them to understand. It takes courage and faith to step out in this kind of partnership, but Isaiah was chosen by Adonai to fulfill this calling and mission.

Imagine with me how hard this would be to comprehend. Hearing but not being able to understand. We know it was not the intent of God for this people to not understand, so it stands to reason why this would be happening in the first place. All I can say at this point is, the eternal God knows what He is wanting to do in the lives of His people, including those in the days of Isaiah. The reception of the message is upon the people. Isaiah's job was to deliver the word of the Lord in the way **Adonai** was directing.

-See but Not Perceive

Second, Adonai informs Isaiah the message he is being commissioned to deliver will be people seeing but not perceiving. I am in no way saying God does not want His

---

[4]Please obtain a copy of Shama, Hearing and Obeying the Voice of God by Mark Burke from Pneumatikos Publishing at www.pneumatikos.com or Passionate for His Purpose at www.passionateforhispurpose.com.

people functioning in their auditory, visual or perceptive giftings and anointings. At this specific point in the history of the people of God, Adonai commissioned these kinds of words to Isaiah. It is quite different, but part of his individual calling before the Lord.

> ***Isaiah 6:9-10*** *...and **see** ye indeed, but **perceive not**. [10] Make the heart of this people fat, and make their ears heavy, and shut their eyes; lest they see with their eyes, and hear with their ears, and understand with their heart, and convert, and be healed.*

I know this sounds like a hard message, and it really is difficult to fully understand the meaning. We must look at this from the eternal mind of God. He recognizes what is going to happen well in advance of . We say in one breath He knows everything, yet when He releases words like this and we see the fulfillment of them, we are stunned in a way. Why? Because it is extremely hard for our human understanding to fully grasp these releases from the eternal perspective, because He sees the end from the beginning; or better yet, the beginning from the end.

He was called to make the heart of the people fat and make their auditory capacities heavy. Additionally, the Scripture says their visual capabilities were going to be shut off, too. The word used for see in this verse speaks of being able to see, or ***ra'ah***, but also knowing the difference between ***towb*** and ***ra***, good or evil/twisted purpose. A question that comes to mind right now is, who is causing the ears to be heavy, eyes to be closed and perceptions to not comprehend? I believe the answer is found in the reception or lack thereof, regarding what God was trying to accomplish in the people. He wants people to hear, see and understand. If an individual chooses not to allow the message to penetrate into their heart, then it will not fall on good ground, but something other than what God intends.

-Conversion and Healing

Adonai wants the people to be converted and healed, or **rapha**, which means to mend or to cure. His desire is conversion and healing for people when they are the cause of their own destruction and desolation.

> **Isaiah 6:9-10** *...and **see** ye indeed, but **perceive not**. [10] Make the heart of this people fat, and make their ears heavy, and shut their eyes; lest they see with their eyes, and hear with their ears, and understand with their heart, and convert, and be healed.*

By conversion, I am not referring to an individual being saved by the blood of Jesus, even though this is the initial beginning point of a new life. Conversion in this context is talking about people returning back to something or someone. The Hebrew word for converted is **shuwb**, and it simply means to turn back. In this case, the desire of **Adonai** is obviously wanting the people to turn back to God. Turn back to what or whom? To return to their God and His intentions and assignments for His people. As this conversion takes place, then healing can come, too.

God can cure anything no matter how awful it looks in the natural realm. He wants to mend and heal, but people need to recognize they have caused their auditory, visual and perceptions to become affected in inappropriate ways. Again, it is not any fault of God. Isaiah was called to a ministry in which these kinds of things would be happening among the people. We need to remember this, because it is important for us today just like it was in the prophetic ministry of Isaiah. People not responding correctly to the message, visual capacities being closed and hearts becoming fat is something that can happen when releasing words and messages of this sort. Look with me at the passage in the New Testament concerning this same insight. Jesus is quoting directly from the Book of Isaiah.

> ***Matthew 13:13-15*** *[13] Therefore speak I to them in parables: because they seeing see not; and hearing they hear not, neither do they understand. [14] And in them is fulfilled the prophecy of Esaias, which saith, By hearing ye shall hear, and shall not understand; and seeing ye shall see, and shall not perceive: [15] For this people's heart is waxed gross, and their ears are dull of hearing, and their eyes they have closed; lest at any time they should see with their eyes, and hear with their ears, and should understand with their heart, and should be converted, and I should heal them.*

The Son of God speaks the same message referenced in Isaiah to His disciples, detailing how people respond to the message and mysteries of the kingdom. He faced it during His earthly ministry, but was also preparing His disciples so they could learn and know what to expect in the coming days. The people chose to have hearts waxed gross, ears dull of hearing, and eyes closed. The desire of the Father and Son is for people to allow conversion and healing to manifest. When this is manifesting, the message and mysteries of the kingdom can begin to be understood, and auditory and visual capacities can and will come alive in the people.

Length of the Assignment: Adonai, How long?

Isaiah continued to hear the words from Adonai regarding the specific details of what would be happening in the people. At some point, he asked a question concerning the duration of the assignment. Specifically, he asked how long do I need to continue with this assignment and mission?

> ***Isaiah 6:11-13*** *¹¹ Then said I, **Lord, [Adonai] how long**? And he answered, Until the **cities** be wasted without inhabitant, and the **houses** without man, and the **land** be utterly desolate, ¹² And the LORD have removed men far away, and there be a great forsaking in the midst of the land. ¹³ But yet in it shall be a tenth, and it shall return, and shall be eaten: as a teil tree, and as an oak, whose substance is in them, when they cast their leaves: so the holy seed shall be the substance thereof.*

This is a question we have all pondered about the mission and assignments we have been given by God to accomplish with Him. It is a legitimate question. How does Adonai answer the question, how long? The answer is rather startling. According to the Scripture, the task at hand was to be fully carried out until cities and houses were wasted without any inhabitants and the land was utterly desolate, or in complete ruin. Yahweh would remove mankind far away. Because of this action, a great forsaking would be in the midst of the land.

The point of all of this is Adonai was giving Isaiah an important task to do, even though it was going to be challenging and extremely difficult. Why would God ask an individual to do this anyway? Obviously, the people had turned their back on God, and He was willing to do whatever it took to bring them back into alignment with His plan and purpose. I believe the great forsaking was indicative of how the people had forsaken God, and this was a demonstration to them of what happens when you turn away from the Lord. We need to remember, the people chose this kind of pathway. This desolation and devastation could have been avoided at all costs if the people had never turned away from God. Yet, in the midst of all the devastation, a tenth, which represents the holy seed, would be preserved in the land.

Like Isaiah, we have a responsibility to be completely committed to whatever mission and assignment Adonai has for us as individuals. Notice with me how he did not get to select his own mission and assignment. He was before the Throne in this dynamic, life-changing place meeting with Adonai. The seraphim were actively involved throughout the entire process. The prophet saw and sensed spiritual things that were remarkable. He witnessed the application of the pure fire from the altar touching his mouth and lips. At any point, Isaiah could have chosen to not partner with what was happening in the spirit, but he willingly humbled and submitted himself to whatever God wanted to do in him. He saw and heard Adonai speaking forth words regarding his individual mission and assignments. What an amazing and challenging scenario that changed his life forever! Be dedicated to the mission and assignments given to you by Adonai.

At this point, I want to transition and refer back to the encounter I was privileged to have around the Throne in heaven. I feel directed to really do my best to capture the perfect atmosphere I felt while in this place. I believe this is essential for us to know, because it keeps our perspective focused on what the Throne is continually involved with day and night. Heaven is so focused on the eternal will of the Father being accomplished on earth as it is in heaven, and as intercessors we need to be reminded of this from time to time.

Chapter 4

Day and Night in Heaven

Heaven Nevers Sleeps nor Rests: Day and Night Heaven Declares Holy, Holy, Holy

During the heavenly encounter I experienced before the Throne, I came to realize some major differences in the way heaven thinks and operates. All of heaven is not affected by the things we are as humans. They function in absolute perfection in accordance with the eternal plan and will of the Father. God, Jesus, Holy Spirit and all the hosts of heaven never sleep nor rest. I felt this in a way I have never experienced before. It is so amazing and gives such a heavenly perspective of how heaven operates and thinks, which is so different from us because we are flesh and blood with a carnal, sinful nature.

This does not mean we cannot function the way heaven does. We can through a divine partnership with God through His Spirit. This journey and relationship begins when we believed in the work Jesus Christ did on the cross on our behalf. As we confess our sins and need for Him, forgiveness and cleansing manifests in us. God then leads us into being filled with the baptism in the Holy Spirit with the initial evidence of speaking in unknown tongues.

What is missing in a lot of Christians is the receiving of the grace gift of divers tongues, which is distinctly different than the initial infilling. The gift is revolutionary in scope in our relationship with God. It is an intercessory gifting to speak directly to God in prayer about His mysteries. Speaking to God is an extraordinary possibility, and this is exactly what is transpiring in the spirit realm. It is the born-again spirit within mankind speaking to God and Jesus, who is continually making intercession before the Throne of God in heaven. This is our link to function in partnering and cooperating with heaven in intercession.

Divers tongues is so essential to communing with God and being a partner with Him. As these languages are spoken forth, it is in accordance with what God is wanting to see done on earth as it is in heaven. Intercession is happening twenty-four hours a day, seven days a week. This is one of the reasons why there is such a major focus upon intercession in our church body, and should be in the body of Christ. Yahweh looks for an intercessor. Christ is at the right hand making intercession for the saints to fulfill the will of God.

> **Isaiah 59:15-16** [15] *Yea, truth faileth; and he that departeth from evil maketh himself a prey: and the* **LORD** *saw it, and it displeased him that there was no judgment.* [16] *And he saw that there was no man, and wondered that there was no intercessor: therefore his arm brought salvation unto him; and his righteousness, it sustained him.*

Jesus Christ is leading the way in this heavenly intercessory ministry. Yahweh's **ra'ah**, vision, or perfect capability to discern the **towb** from the **ra**, is looking for truth, judgment, and intercessors. During the days of Isaiah, He was looking for a man to partner as an intercessor, and He is still looking for individuals to rise up as intercessors in our day. Christ is continually making intercession in heaven for the saints in accordance with the will of God.

Romans 8:26-27 *²⁶ Likewise the Spirit also helpeth our infirmities: for we know not what we should pray for as we ought: but the Spirit itself maketh intercession for us with groanings which cannot be uttered. ²⁷ And he that searcheth the hearts knoweth what is the mind of the Spirit, because he maketh **intercession for the saints according to the will of God**.*

Romans 8:34 *³⁴ Who is he that condemneth? It is **Christ** that died, yea rather, that is risen again, who is even at the right hand of God, who also **maketh intercession for us**.*

I am saying all of this about intercession to show the connective of what is happening in the spirit of man when praying in unknown and divers tongues. We are joining through partnership by the Spirit with Christ who is making intercession at the right hand of God. This is our placement in heaven now. It is not just in the sweet by and by as some would think. Humans were created to function in this way before God. Perfect intercessory exchanges are taking place as we pray in the spirit. Diverse languages coming out of our spirit indicate lots of insight, and revelation is being spoken forth concerning the mysteries. As we commit to interceding in this way, understandings will come. Paul said we need to pray with our spirit, and we need to continue to pray with the understanding.

1 Corinthians 14:15 *15 What is it then? I will **pray with the spirit**, and I will **pray with the understanding** also: I will sing with the spirit, and I will sing with the understanding also.*

Interceding in the spirit is essential for individuals and churches. We need to commune with God by praying with the spirit and praying with our understanding regarding what is happening in the spirit. Paul knew this in his life and is restating this to the church at Corinth and to us as well. Pray and understand at the same time. It is something that can be done and can be very fruitful. We can also sing with the spirit and with the understanding, too. Life in the spirit with God is completely satisfying and fulfilling. Nothing else on this earth compares.

Yahweh Does Not Slumber or Sleep

The Bible teaches us a lot about spiritual things that are very much relevant in our day. One of these realities is how the Word of God describes Yahweh as not sleeping nor slumbering.

> ***Psalm 121:1-8*** *[1] I will lift up mine eyes unto the hills, from whence cometh my help. [2] My help cometh from the **LORD**, **[Yahweh]** which made heaven and earth. [3] He will not suffer thy foot to be moved: he that keepeth thee will **not slumber**. [4] Behold, he that keepeth Israel shall **neither slumber** nor **sleep**. [5] The LORD is thy keeper: the LORD is thy shade upon thy right hand. [6] The sun shall not smite thee by day, nor the moon by night. [7] The LORD shall preserve thee from all evil: he shall preserve thy soul. [8] The LORD shall preserve thy going out and thy coming in from this time forth, and even for evermore.*

These are two ways, as human beings, we are very different from **Yahweh**. This is the name that speaks of the eternal plan of God. As humans we become tired from the various activities throughout our day. We expend lots of energy when exercising and afterwards are really physically and mentally drained from the workout. At some point, we need to sleep in order to be rejuvenated for the next day and what lies ahead.

Sleep is necessary for us as humans to function properly. A lack of sleep can result in an individual being irritable and lead to not being able to think and focus clearly. There are many other negative aspects to sleep deprivation, but you get the point. Sleep, however, is not one of the myriad activities in heaven.

With **Yahweh**, or relating to any person in the Godhead, or being, they do not need sleep. Heaven never sleeps. The eternal will and plan is always the focal point of their existence. Like the psalmist says, we need to lift up our visionary capacities to the hills because our help comes from **Yahweh**, or His eternal plan. He made heaven and earth. To help in this verse is a reference which means He wants to come to our aid, protect, and surround His people. He is the One who will surround, protect, and come to our aid. It is our choice where we look, though. Let us all commit to lifting up our eyes to the hills which clearly elevates our vision to not be focused on the things of this earth. Lift up your eyes because our help comes from above. We will be tempted to look down at our circumstances and surroundings; but when this happens, may we never forget to lift up our vision towards heaven. True and eternal help comes from **Yahweh**.

Another startling fact about the eternal plan, or **Yahweh**, is He does not slumber. Sleep and slumber are very much different. To be asleep you are completely in a state of not waking up. On the other hand, slumbering is when you are slumbering or in a state of drowsiness. You are awake, but in a point of feeling being so drowsy you are inactive. Yahweh is neither of these two things. This goes along with the reality that heaven does not sleep nor slumber. Yahweh is completely aware and awake at all times, passionately focusing on what needs to be accomplished in heaven. Not just **Yahweh**, but all of heaven is this way. The Father, Son, Holy Spirit, and the angelic do not need sleep, and they definitely do not get so drowsy to the point of becoming inactive.

Yahweh, or His eternal plan, is spoken of in the above passage as being our keeper, shade, preserver from all evil, or *ra,* which is twisted purpose and preservation of our going out and coming in now and in the future. This Psalm is packed with incredible revelation concerning the essence of *Yahweh* and how He will help to preserve those functioning in the eternal plan. What magnificent promises!

Four Beasts: Declare Holy, Holy, Holy

God is so desirous of people knowing Him and functioning in accordance with His design in mind. While I was interceding in the spirit, I was made aware of being around the Throne of God in heaven, and particularly the four beasts. It was very similar to what John experienced as he was granted access through a door, or *thyra,* which refers to a spiritual access point into heaven. Doorways in the spirit are also known as portals, or spiritual openings. God grants access in and out of these to individuals as He sees fit.

> *Revelation 4:1* *[1] After this I looked, and, behold, **a door was opened in heaven**: [Access Granted into Heaven] and the first voice which I heard was as it were of a trumpet talking with me; which said, Come up hither, and I will shew thee things which must be hereafter.*

Immediate Access into Heaven

As I felt a surge in my spirit and began interceding in diversities of tongues, my languages transitioned into declaring the words holy, holy, holy in a rapid continuance fashion. I must say, this is not something that can be manufactured. When the spirit of an intercessor is deep in the spirit realm, our spirits can be speaking in lots of languages and doing a lot of things, but our mind sometimes is not fruitful or fully understanding what is occurring in the spirit. This is not always the case, though. , As we pray in the spirit, we need to pray for the understanding, too. My mind was in a state of utter astonishment as this was happening. At one point, I even remembering thinking about trying to force myself to stop or bring some type of change, but I was unable to do anything else. My spirit just continued declaring with the four beasts and angelic holy, holy, holy or saint, saint, saint. I can remember the above verses coming to my mind, which caused my mind to become fruitful.

> ***Revelation 4:8-9*** *[8] And the four beasts had each of them six wings about him; and they were full of eyes within: and they rest not day and night, saying, Holy, holy, holy, Lord God Almighty, which was, and is, and is to come. [9] And when those beasts give glory and honour and thanks to him that sat on the throne, who liveth for ever and ever,*

As my spirit was praying, I just knew I was near the four beasts who are described in the Scripture above. My mind was fully aware of what was transpiring, but my spirit seemed to be on autopilot as I was encountering various activities and spirit beings in heaven. I was so overwhelmed, in a good way, as this was taking place in my spirit and mind. God can do these kinds of things in us if we will allow Him to cause our spirit to come alive in this way. He created our spirit man to commune and function with Him in heaven now. We are to be functioning from our place at the right hand alongside Jesus in heaven now.

Like John, God can and does allow access into heaven in this same manner today. I know our carnal mind and other thought patterns will say otherwise. We need to believe the Bible for what it says and not accept only the parts we are willing to embrace. It should not be this way. God is the same yesterday, today and forever and does not change. This brings me to a good question. Who has changed, then? God? This is absurd to even ponder. Human beings are the ones who are constantly not willing to believe spiritual things founded upon the Scripture.

For a very long time, I had no idea these spiritual things could happen in me either. All I remember was desperate for more of Him. I tried to find this in a lot of churches and other ungodly ways. Everywhere my wife and I seemed to go to church, something was missing. That forever changed the moment we stepped into the body at The Father's Church. I specifically remember feeling the atmosphere walking in and even knew at that point it was much different. That day would earmark the beginning of a new journey in Him that has been absolutely remarkable. The grace gift of divers tongues was activated in me. It is this spiritual gift that propelled me forward in the spirit in experiencing and knowing God in much deeper ways.

Before we move on to some other important things that happened in the spirit to me, I want to focus specifically on some key points in the above passage from the Book of Revelation. It is not my intention to explain all the details, but to simply highlight certain things in the spirit realm that were happening during this time at the Throne.

In the Spirit at the Throne

-On the Throne

While in the spirit, John begins to see God sitting upon the Throne that looked like a jasper and sardine stone.

> ***Revelation 4:2-3*** *² And immediately **I was in the spirit**: and, behold, **a throne was set in heaven**, and one sat on the throne. ³And he that sat was to look upon like a jasper and a sardine stone:*

As John is functioning as a human being in the spirit realm at the Throne, it is very interesting to see how the Spirit is impressing upon him to describe what he is sensing and seeing at the Throne in heaven. He used terminology such as on, in the midst and around about, out of, and before the Throne of God. He is doing his very best to give us directional perspective. In order to help us with a visual, I have put the headings together like they are described in this passage in hopes it will help us have a much better grasp of what is transpiring at the Throne during the timeframe in which John was alive.

-In the Midst and Round About the Throne

-A Rainbow

A rainbow, or the Seven Spirits of God, is described as round about the Throne. While looking at this phenomenal scene, the Throne was like an emerald green, which speaks of the Spirit of Prophecy.[5] This was a picture of what God was depicting at this point for John to witness and see. The Throne of God can depict all the seven different dimensions of the Seven Spirits of God. It just so happened to be resembling what God was doing at that specific time.

> **Revelation 4:3** *...and there was a rainbow round about the throne, in sight like unto an emerald.*

Each time a reference is made about something or someone being around about the Throne, it is the Greek word **kyklothen** is used, meaning from the circle or to be all around. All around what, you might ask? A rainbow all around or

---

[5] Please obtain a copy of Heaven, by Ron Crawford from Pneumatikos Publishing at www.pneumatikos.com.

circling the Throne of God. The rainbow speaks of the establishment of His covenant for the earth, and is also a reference to the seven dimensions of His personality, or Seven Spirits of God.[6]

-24 Seats and 24 Elders

Round about the Throne are twenty-four seats, which represent authority and power, and in these seats were twenty-four elders, or mature ones. They are described as clothed in white raiment with crowns of gold on their head. The clothing being worn represents the fullness of the ways of God, or the saintly white garments.

> ***Revelation 4:4*** *[4] And **round about the throne** were four and twenty seats: and upon the seats I saw four and twenty elders sitting, clothed in white raiment; and they had on their heads crowns of gold.*

-The Four Beasts

In the midst and round about, or encircling the Throne, are spirit beings known as the four beasts. They are vividly described by John as being full of eyes before and behind. They are described as appearing like a lion, calf, face of a man, a flying eagle. I am in no way going to address specifics about these incredible beings in heaven. I do want to focus on some of their behavior and how they function at the Throne.

> ***Revelation 4:6-11*** *...**in the midst of the throne**, and **round about the throne**, were four beasts full of eyes before and behind. [7] And the first beast was*

---

[6] Please obtain a copy of Manual of the Seven Spirits, by Ron Crawford from Pneumatikos Publishing at www.pneumatikos.com.

*like a lion, and the second beast like a calf, and the third beast had a face as a man, and the fourth beast was like a flying eagle. [8] And the **four beasts** had each of them six wings about him; and they were **full of eyes within**: and **they rest not day and night, saying, Holy, holy, holy, Lord God Almighty, which was, and is, and is to come**. [9] And when those beasts give glory and honour and thanks to him that sat on the throne, who liveth for ever and ever, [10] The four and twenty elders fall down before him that sat on the throne, and worship him that liveth for ever and ever, and cast their crowns before the throne, saying, [11] Thou art worthy, O Lord, to receive glory and honour and power: for thou hast created all things, and for thy pleasure they are and were created.*

Their visionary capabilities are identified as being full of eyes within, before and behind. To me, this speaks of what they see and how they are created to function and move with God and those in partnership with the Lord. It seems their duties are focused on the ways of God which is why they are spoken of with eyes within, in front of and from the back. Eyes inside and all around focusing on the intents of the heart of God.[7]

-No Rest Day or Night

The four beasts are devoted in their duties and are spoken of as not resting day or night. The Greek word for rest in this verse is **anapausis**, which means intermission or recreation. In other words, the four beasts, and all of heaven, do not need

---

[7] Please obtain a copy of Chariot of the Cherubim, by Ron Crawford from Pneumatikos Publishing at www.pneumatikos.com.

times of intermission or recreation in the sense like humans do. The Bible is very clear; they do not ever "rest," as they are continuously working day and night to accomplish the intents and desires of God. No rest is needed in heaven, because it is a place of total perfection.

By contrast, as human beings we get tired and need to rest to become refreshed and reinvigorated for the next day. We get extremely exhausted mentally and physically from the various activities and tasks of the day. As I was privileged to experience encountering the four beasts, I was greatly moved in my spirit by the feeling and perfect atmosphere of heaven and the devotion of these spiritual beings. There have been additional interactions that have all left me feeling totally stunned by absolute perfect dedication and devotion to the eternal will and plan of God.

-Seeing and Hearing the Words of the Four Beasts: Come and See

As John encountered the Lamb opening the seals, his seer and auditory abilities allowed him to see and hear the voice and words of what the beasts were saying to him. All four beasts functioned in perfect unison in their declaration as they declare, "Come and see." I have been around these beings recently during times of intercession at the Throne and heard the words "see." These are invitations to see and hear what God is speaking forth. The passage listed below speaks of their declarations as the Lamb opens the four seals.

> ***Revelation 6:1-8***   *[1] And **I saw** when the Lamb opened one of the seals, and **I heard**, as it were the noise of thunder, **one of the four beasts saying, Come and see**. 2 And I saw, and behold a white horse: and he that sat on him had a bow; and a crown was given unto him: and he went forth conquering, and to conquer. 3 And when he had*

*opened the second seal, I heard the **second beast say, Come and see**. 4 And there went out another horse that was red: and power was given to him that sat thereon to take peace from the earth, and that they should kill one another: and there was given unto him a great sword. 5 And when he had opened the third seal, **I heard the third beast say, Come and see**. And I beheld, and lo a black horse; and he that sat on him had a pair of balances in his hand. 6 And I heard a voice in the midst of the four beasts say, A measure of wheat for a penny, and three measures of barley for a penny; and see thou hurt not the oil and the wine. 7 And when he had opened the fourth seal, **I heard the voice of the fourth beast say, Come and see**. 8 And I looked, and behold a pale horse: and his name that sat on him was Death, and Hell followed with him. And power was given unto them over the fourth part of the earth, to kill with sword, and with hunger, and with death, and with the beasts of the earth.*

-The Lamb

John was granted access to see and witness incredible things in the spirit realm. In this case, he is giving powerful insights into how an individual can be carried away in the spirit and be at the Throne. While he is at the Throne in Revelation 7, he speaks about the concept and reality of the Lamp being in the midst of the Throne providing nourishment much like a shepherd would to the flock for these individuals, and leading or showing the way to living fountains of waters. Let us look at the passage together.

Revelation 7:13-17 *¹³ And **one of the elders answered, saying unto me**, [John] What are these which are arrayed in white robes? and whence* *came they? [14] And **I said unto him**, [elder] Sir, thou knowest. And **he [elder] said to me**, These are they which came out of great tribulation, and have washed their robes, and made them white in the blood of the Lamb. [15] Therefore are they before the **throne of God**, and serve him **day and night in his temple**: and he that sitteth on the throne shall dwell among them. [16] They shall hunger no more, neither thirst any more; neither shall the sun light on them, nor any heat. [17] **For the Lamb which is in the midst of the throne** shall **feed** them, and shall **lead** them unto living fountains of waters: and God shall wipe away all tears from their eyes.*

John, while in the spirit before the Throne, encounters one of the elders speaking to him. He asked him several questions, and it appears John does not know the answers. He defers giving any answers and then speaks to this elder by saying, "You know the answer." At this point, some powerful insights are given to John as the elder in heaven answers the two questions he initially was asking John about earlier. God can do these kinds of things as we are functioning in the spirit realm. I am only reporting what is revealed in the Scripture.

My intent as we study this passage together is to look at the various activities and insights about the Throne of God and what is taking place. I am not suggesting an eschatological discussion here, but rather focusing on the important principles and truths in these verses. The first truth is the individuals are identified as coming out of the great tribulation, which is referring to tremendous points of great warfare. Their robes are said to be washed and made white in the blood of the Lamb, which indicates intense times of warfare. The garments we wear can become stained or soiled by the battle. It is necessary for this kind of washing in the blood to occur. As a result, the same garments are made white.

Second, these same individuals are spoken of as being before the Throne of God. God called an individual, whose name is John, to enter into heavenly realms. He witnesses these things and is giving us details of how individuals today can be before the Throne. It is not just something for John to experience. We are seated in heavenly places at the right hand of God.

A third insight is the same individuals are in service in the heavenly temple day and night. Lest we forget the context of the biblical text, this is all happening in the spirit realm before the Throne (Revelation 7:9-12). This elder is specifically telling John how individuals can function in heaven and in the heavenly temple in an ongoing fashion. In this type of service, the Scripture clearly reveals these mighty ones will have no more hunger, thirst, neither will sun or heat light upon them. The Lamb will dwell, feed and lead these ones into partaking of the living fountains of waters, and God will wipe, or smear out or completely obliterate, all tears from their eyes.

These warriors are serving, or *latreuo*, which means to minister to God and render homage to Him. The place where this service is transpiring is in the heavenly temple. He uses terms like day and night, which speaks of it being done on a continual basis. God is teaching us what it means to walk and live in the spirit, or His breath. What amazing insights and revelations in the Word of God!

-Out of the Throne

Out of the Throne there are lightnings, thunderings, voices and seven lamps of fire burning before the Throne. The Bible identified these lamps as the Seven Spirits of God, or the ways of God. There are a lot of spiritual activities taking place before the Throne. The beauty of this is God is extending invitations for His creation to come up into this incredible place to partner with what He is wanting to accomplish on earth as it is in heaven.

> ***Revelation 4:5*** *⁵ And **out of the throne** proceeded lightnings and thunderings and voices: and there were seven lamps of fire burning before the throne, which are the seven Spirits of God.*

-Before the Throne

Positioned before the Throne is a sea of glass which looks like crystal. I am only making reference to the various things that are mentioned in Revelation 4. If you would like to know more about the sea of glass, you can obtain a copy of Pastor Ron Crawford's book titled Heaven. I have made reference to it previously in one of the footnotes.

> ***Revelation 4:6*** *⁶And before the throne there was a sea of glass like unto crystal: and in the midst of the throne,...*

Heavenly experiences like I have been writing about are intended for specific purposes in mind. God is not just giving us encounters without a reason. They are extended to us so we can become trusted partners with His Spirit and what is transpiring on His eternal timeline. Sometimes it is so difficult to explain what is seen, heard, and felt during these life-changing experiences before the Throne in heaven. It is my prayer that God would continue to open the eyes of our understanding and help us explain these powerful insights.

As I have previously stated, God and all of heaven are continuously working in establishing and partnering with intercessors for His eternal will and plan to done on earth as it is in heaven. On the other hand, Satan and his demonic forces are also working in the same manner to attempt to stop saints and intercessors from partnering with God. In the next section, we will look at the reality of how the demonic realm is actively functioning day and night to prevent, hinder and destroy what God is wanting to accomplish in the earth. Some of his objectives are to steal, kill and destroy.

Chapter 5

Day and Night in the Demonic Realm

The Bible is very clear in describing things that are happening in the spirit realm. For so many years, I knew this reality existed and had experienced it to a certain degree, but nothing like God is allowing me to walk in today. The relational experiences afford us many ways to commune and fellowship with God in the spirit and truth; and as this happens, His Spirit begins to reveal things to us as we continue to devote ourselves to intercession. Insights and revelations are shared in His timing and His choosing.

Heaven is relentless on enforcing the plan and will of God on earth as it in heaven. On the other hand, we need to not be ignorant of the enemy and his forces having a twisted, demonic passion to see the destruction and deception of the plan and will of God. We need those who are spiritually trained to recognize the devices of the enemy.

2 Corinthians 2:11 *[11] Lest Satan should get an advantage of us: for we are not ignorant of his devices.*

Satan has a twisted way of thinking as it relates to taking advantage and attempting to keep individuals in an ***agnoeo*** state that leads to not recognizing his devices. To be ***agoneo*** refers to not knowing through lack of information or intelligence, or just to ignore through disinclination. The enemy wants mankind to be disinclined, disinterested, or ignoring his satanic devices. This does not mean we focus on him, but the people of God need to be aware of various strategies and devices. The Greek word used for devices in this verse is ***noema,*** which speaks of the perceptions, purpose and intellectual disposition of our enemy. After Lucifer fell from his perfect state, his spiritual perceptions, purpose and way of thinking became demonically filled with corruption. He is on the move attempting to establish his demonic, twisted purpose and looking for willing partners to join with him and his forces.

As I was studying this verse, my spirit was being drawn to the opposite of ***agnoeo,*** which is ***noeo.*** If Satan wants individuals to remain in a state of ignorance, then God is wanting His people to function in ***noeo,*** which is a reference of using the mind for comprehension and meaning. ,By looking at the direct opposite of ***agnoeo,*** we glean the intent and desire of God for us to gain understanding. We are not to be ***agnoeo,*** but comprehending and discerning the twisted intentions and tactics of Satan. Again, we do not fixate on the enemy, but we do need to recognize what he is trying to do to get an advantage against us.

It is so important for us as intercessors to continually be coming before the Throne of God in heaven to allow the Spirit of God to help us. His Spirit is perfect and can assist us to think as a son and function in all His perfect ways. We need to remember this when things are good or not so good. God is always present, and we just need to draw nigh, and He will draw nigh to us.

In the next section of the writing, my intent is to show how the enemy and his fallen angels are at work day and night, too. Their agenda is to focused on direct opposition to what God is accomplishing through His sons. They speak lies and deception and will do whatever it takes to keep people from partnering with God in establishing heaven on earth.

The Accuser of the Brethren

The Bible speaks a great deal about Satan and his twisted desires to bring deception into the lives of individuals and into the world. He has demonic intentions to bring destruction and death. John spoke about the accuser of the brethren in the Book of Revelation.

> ***Revelation 12:7-9*** *⁷ And there was war in heaven:* ***Michael*** *and* ***his angels*** *fought against the dragon; and the dragon fought and his angels, ⁸ And prevailed not; neither was their place found any more in heaven. ⁹ And the great dragon was cast out, that old serpent, called the Devil, and Satan, which* ***deceiveth the whole world****: he was cast out into the earth, and his angels were cast out with him.*

To Deceive the Whole World

The above passage is one warfare and speaks about Michael and his angels fighting against the great dragon and his angels. As this warfare is happening in the spirit, the Bible teaches us that Satan and his demonic forces were not able to prevail against the warriors and the angelic of Michael. There are several important realities the Holy Spirit quickened to me about the old serpent. One is about his overall objective is to deceive the whole world. To deceive means to cause people to stray away from something. It stems from the root word ***planos***, which simply refers to an imposter or misleader. He is always trying to impose and mislead the people, churches and nations all across the world. According to the dictionary definition, an imposter is one who practices deception under an assumed character, identity or name. This is a true description of the enemy. He is also trying to mislead, or cause people to lead or guide in a wrong manner which leads down a pathway of error. In other words, he wants to lead us in the wrong direction.

Notice with me the extent of Satan's deception. He is focused on releasing evil into the world. This is in direct opposition to God calling us to go into all the world to minister the gospel of the kingdom and teach all nations. According to the biblical text, at some point in this intense warfare battle, he and his angels were unable to prevail against the mighty angelic forces of the Lord and were cast out. As this happens, John said he heard a loud voice from heaven making declarations including identifying Satan as the accuser of the brethren.

> ***Revelation 12:10-11*** *[10] And I heard a loud voice saying in heaven, Now is come salvation, and strength, and the kingdom of our God, and the power of his Christ: for **the accuser of our brethren is cast down, which accused them before our God day and night**. [11] And they overcame him by the blood of the Lamb, and by the word of their testimony; and they loved not their lives unto the death.*

The Scripture says our enemy, Satan, is in the spirit realm making accusations against the brethren before God. Accusations are tactics he attempts to use against the people of God. We must be aware of this taking place in the spirit because it can help us as we are functioning in spirit and truth. As was previously mentioned, we do not need to be disinterested, ignore or be disinclined to the satanic devices. For him to accuse in this way, it just means he is trying to charge us with an offence before God. God is in charge, not the enemy. We need to know this deep in our thoughts. God is for us, not against us.

Day and Night

In addition to Satan being identified as the accuser of the brethren, the Bible tells us when these accusatory words are being addressed before God, he is making these defaming remarks day and night. When Lucifer was expelled from his perfect estate, he and one-third of the angelic forces he convinced to go with him became corrupt and limited in what they could accomplish and do in the spirit and in the earth. They do not have a limitless supply. They cannot be in every place all the time. God is omnipresent and has limitless resources, not the enemy.

Why am I saying all this anyway? I am trying to paint a picture for all of us regarding the demonically driven desire of Satan and his fallen ones to prevent the people of God from moving forward in taking dominion. They never cease, day or night, in this twisted pursuit. This should stir the saints to continually go before God in intercession, not allowing anything we face to prevent us from seeking the thoughts and heart of God. Satan is still a murderer, or man killer, from the beginning. He does not like that God is partnering with His saints and sons.

Something I want to bring back to your attention are the four beasts and all of heaven that never rest and are continuously fulfilling the eternal will and plan of God . There are two kingdoms involved in this equation, that they are direct opposites. On one side is the kingdom of God, and on the opposing side is the kingdom of Satan. God will ultimately prevail. His kingdom is far above and greater than any other kingdom. He has all power and authority, not the enemy.

To me, the reality of Satan working in the day-and-night fashion gives us incredible insight into the spirit realm and how he is operating continuously. This should ignite a renewed commitment and passion in us to pursue God with all our might. As human beings, we can be prone to allow the way we feel to dictate what we do. We are flesh and blood, but we need to remember how demonically driven our enemy is and continue to push forward in spending time before God in intercessory prayer. God knows exactly every detail about us, even when we do not feel like we have a grasp on what He is doing in our lives. He knows the number of hairs on our heads, which speaks of the immense detail He knows about us individually. God is for us, and the enemy is against us, plotting his evil plans and accusations. We need to be done with lesser things and be laser focused and driven in pursuing hard after the heart of God.

Overcoming

How are we instructed to overcome these accusations being proclaimed before God? First, we overcome the enemy by the cleansing and forgiving power of the blood of the Lamb. Second, by the word, or *logos*, or our testimony. As we continue to become martyrs to self and allow the desires and intents of our Father to be known, we partner with what He is saying and doing. This becomes part of the word of our testimony. ***Logos*** focuses on foundational purpose, and it was with God in the very beginning (John 1:1-2). Of course, grace is also involved in overcoming, but this verse focuses on the blood and the word of our testimony, which are very important and powerful as we partner with God in what He wants to accomplish within us.

Revelation 12:11 [11] And they overcame him by the blood of the Lamb, and by the word of their testimony; and they loved not their lives unto the death.

The Accuser Accuses Job: Before the Sons of God and Yahweh

Job is one individual that comes to mind regarding Satan's attempt to get him to turn away from serving God. This entire passage must be viewed from the perspective of God knowing the beginning from the end. He knew the outcome; Job would ultimately triumph and be an overcomer.

> ***Job 1:6-7*** *⁶ Now there was a day when the **sons of God** came to present themselves before the LORD, and **Satan came** also among them. ⁷ And the **LORD said unto Satan**, Whence comest thou? Then **Satan answered the LORD**, and said, From going to and fro in the earth, and from walking up and down in it.*

I have to admit some happenings in this passage are a bit perplexing to the carnal mind. The heavenly scene includes Yahweh, angelic sons of God, and Satan. This is an interesting cast of beings. I would think the angelic sons of God should only be permitted, but Yahweh allowed Satan to come into this heavenly place. From a human perspective, this sounds a bit crazy, if you ask me. Why would God allow the one who rebelled to come into the very presence of Yahweh, or His plan? God oversees everything and determines if these kinds of interactions are allowed by Him, or not. This was one of these situations. It does not make sense to our carnal way of thinking. Our carnality is at enmity with the things of the Spirit. God knew who Job was and how he would respond and act; He was not setting him up for failure or defeat. Read the collection of verses below which speak about how God thought and felt towards Job.

> ***Job 1:1-3*** *¹ There was a man in the land of Uz, whose name was Job; and that man was **perfect***

***and upright, and one that feared God, and eschewed evil.** 2 And there were born unto him seven sons and three daughters. 3 His substance also was seven thousand sheep, and three thousand camels, and five hundred yoke of oxen, and five hundred she asses, and a very great household; so that this man was the **greatest of all the men of the east**.*

Quite the contrary, Elohim would be walking with Job, which would result in phenomenal provisions and blessings. We must submit our ways of thinking and doing to His thoughts and ways. His Spirit desires to transform us in every way. God knew Job was perfect and upright, and feared God, or **Elohim**, which represents His heart and that he was one who turned off **ra**, or twisted purpose. Like Job, God knows us very deeply, and nothing is hidden from His eyes of fire and vision. In addition, he was spoken of as the greatest of all the men of the east. He was blessed with cattle and had a very great household. He was a remarkable individual before the heart of God.

On this specific day, with the angelic sons of God and Satan present, Yahweh initiates the conversation by addressing Satan with a specific question: Where are you coming from? God already knew the answer to this question, because He is all-knowing. God seems to address people, as in this case, with questions. Satan responds with an answer in a two-fold manner. First, he states he has been operating to and fro in the earth. Second, he is depicted as walking up and down in the earth. This is contrasted with his original purpose, before he rebelled, in that God created him to walk up and down in the midst of the stones of fire. Going to and fro and up and down in the earth speaks of the various maneuverings of the enemy. He is very much active in these various directional dimensions in the spirit realm.

I am amazed by this entire spiritual encounter, but it is a visual representation of how the accuser of the brethren makes accusations of those who are functioning like Job. Those moving in the spirit as sons of God will be accused in a similar fashion. We do not need to fear, because Yahweh is near and knows the end from the beginning. This must be our mindset. Otherwise, we will be confused and not really assured the Lord has our best interest in mind. He knows all the plans He has for each of us. The dialogue between Yahweh and Satan reveals some powerful insights and revelations into how Yahweh and Satan function.

Yahweh continues the dialogue by asking Satan another question: Have you considered my servant Job…,and many other things about who Job was in Him. I think this is so incredible. This gives us specific details of how Yahweh thought about Job. As I am typing these words, my mind and spirit are overwhelmed by what is spoken forth about an individual who is functioning before Yahweh. As we look at this together, focus your attention on the content of all that Yahweh, or His eternal plan, is communicating about Job.

Yahweh's Servant: Have You Considered My Servant Job?

Yahweh proceeds to ask the enemy a question centered around the identity of Job. He says, have you considered my servant Job. To be called a servant of Yahweh, or His plan, is wonderful. What a powerful declaration! This resonates with me and it should in you, too. We are called, like Job, to be servants of the plan of God.

> ***Job 1:8*** *And the **LORD said** unto Satan, Hast thou considered my servant Job, that there is none like him in the earth, a perfect and an upright man, one*

*that **feareth God, [Elohim]** and **escheweth evil**? [ra]*

Yahweh Says

Notice with me how Yahweh is speaking on behalf of His servant directly to Satan. This is completely astounding to me. It is not Job speaking to the enemy about the purpose and plan of God., Yahweh is making these statements concerning the plan and purpose of Job. To be a servant is referring to an individual who is actively involved in and enslaved to something or someone. Job is enslaved to Yahweh, or the eternal plan. This is still the intent of God today for His people to be slaves to His plan and purpose. This gives great explanation as to why Satan is involved in this spiritual scenario in the spirit realm. Those who are actively enslaved to the plan and purpose of God will be opposed by the enemy and his forces. It is just part of the process in partnership with Yahweh. It does not mean our Father has left or abandoned us in this process.

Yahweh speaks on behalf of Job by speaking to Satan about the heart and identity of the man of God. He is identified as none like him in the earth, perfect, upright, fearing God. This is astounding to me. Yahweh releases these incredible words regarding His plan and purpose. A lot could be mentioned here about this detailing. We must be those who are perfect, or complete, and upright before God. Like Job, we need to be those who have reverential fear for God, or Elohim, which speaks of the things of His heart. In addition, he was spoken of as eschewing evil, or an individual who turned off anything associated with twisted purpose. This is what the people of God are supposed to be in this hour.

These are powerful words, and we must recognize the immense gravity of what is being communicated about an individual that is walking like Job. He was definitely a person of great value from Yahweh's and Satan's perspectives. Of course, the enemy was accusing him of serving the plan of God for all the wrong reasons. What was Satan really thinking in leveling these kinds of accusatory words anyway? Does he think Yahweh did not know what was in the heart of Job? It just reveals how demonically intent he is in his evil pursuits of trying to get individuals in a Job-like walk to curse the plan of God. This was his twisted purpose.

Was this spiritual scenario part of the plan of God for Job? I know this sounds bizarre, but it was definitely allowed to take place by Yahweh. Could God have stopped this from happening? We all know this answer. He can do anything He wants. Yet, His eternal plan and purpose determined this was being allowed, even though it would feel and look really bad in the natural realm. God sees things from a different perspective than we do as humans. Nothing is hidden from Him. All things work out for the good to those who are functioning in the ***agape*** and are called according to His purpose.

Accusation of Satan: Serving Yahweh Because of All the Blessing

The next part in this conversation between Yahweh and Satan is loaded with the intents and thoughts of the enemy. We need to focus on the content of what is being released by him. In doing so, we can glean the twistedness of the way he thinks towards those walking like Job. As we look into the words of Satan, we should gain a greater measure of understanding in the inner mindset and workings of the enemy. On the other hand, we can also see some astounding insights into godly things.

Satan's Questions to Yahweh

Question 1: Does Job fear God for nought?

Satan speaks several more questions to Yahweh concerning Job. The first question is strategically focused on accusing him for Job fearing God, or His heart, for nought.

> ***Job 1:9*** *⁹ Then **Satan answered the LORD**, and said, Doth Job fear God for nought?*

The enemy is very crafty and more subtle than any other creature that was made, and will attempt to distort and misrepresent. He will twist things against those moving and functioning in a Job-like manner. As saints, we need to be aware and not ignorant of his strategies. If he thinks he can somehow trick or convince God in this way, he must think again. Our Father already knows everything and has unlimited knowledge and power about all the details of our individual walk before the Throne in heaven.

Question 2: The Hedge of Yahweh (His Plan)

The second topic the enemy brought before Yahweh was about his knowledge regarding the hedge of protection that was upon Job, his house, and all that he had on every side. What a demonic insight coming from the mouth of the enemy! We need to not be ignorant of his devices.

> ***Job 1:10*** *...thou hast blessed the work of his hands, and his substance is increased in the land.*

Satan just spoke of a protective measure surrounding the man of God. The limited knowledge the enemy has is very clear in this passage, but he still knows certain things because he used to be perfect in all his ways until iniquity was found in him. At that specific time, he was removed from a place of perfection and no longer functioned in this way. He now moves in corruption, deception, seduction, lies and much more as he goes, up and down, and to fro in the earth. He recognizes the hedge of Yahweh is impenetrable unless it is removed by Him. This is a powerful revelation concerning how the plan of Yahweh is surrounding those who are functioning in His eternal plan. As saints and intercessors, we must always keep this at the forefront of our mind.

The enemy also revealed knowing about how Yahweh had blessed the work of his hands and his substance being increased in the land. I am not glorifying Satan by any means, but he is not unknowledgeable as some voices in this world say. He has some corrupted abilities to know limited things about individuals. In this case, he recognized the blessing and increase in the life of Job. Some questions we might have regarding these kinds of things happening to individuals we will never fully understand; we must continue to trust the eternal plan and purpose of God, because nothing is allowed without His approval.

Objective of Satan: Cursing Yahweh, or His Eternal Plan

Satan and his demonic teammates are always attempting to bring deception into this world. He maneuvers day and night to fulfill his evil plan and purpose. So, what is his objective in accusing Job? Let's look at the verses below, which reveal the ultimate intent of the enemy in the life of Job.

> ***Job 1:11*** *[11] But put forth thine hand now, and touch all that he hath, and he will **curse thee to thy face**.*

First, Satan speaks to Yahweh by saying, if you will put forth your hand and touch all that he has, Job will curse thee to your face. His intent was so twisted and demonic. I am not suggesting we welcome this kind of spiritual attack at all. I am saying we need to be aware of what the enemy is doing in the spiritual realm in making these kinds of destructive remarks to Yahweh, or His eternal plan. Our enemy wants us to curse Yahweh, releasing words that are damning to God's eternal plan and purpose. Instead of cursing the face, which means to turn, we need to release and speak blessing as it relates to His plan and purpose. We need to remember Yahweh is still turned in our direction, even when things may not be very pleasant. He allows these kinds of occurrences to strengthen us and to empower us to overcome in grace . The accusation in Verse 11 reveals how the enemy is thinking towards Job. He is demonically driven to accuse Job of only serving Yahweh because of the blessings bestowed upon him.

This can be extremely challenging, especially in the midst of intense spiritual warfare. Lest we forget, remember the context of this passage. This is all happening in the spirit. Job is soon to see and feel many different things manifesting in the physical realm. He was a chosen servant of Yahweh. What happens next in this conversation between Yahweh and Satan? It is very difficult to understand from a human perspective.

Yahweh Says: You Have Access to Job and All That He Has

The conversation continues between Yahweh and Satan. I know what I am about to say does not make any sense to the carnal mind, but the Bible is very clear of what Yahweh permits the enemy to do.

Job 1:12 *[12] And the **LORD said unto Satan**, Behold, all that he hath is in thy power; only upon himself put not forth thine hand. **[Yahweh Has the***

*Ultimate Say] So **Satan went forth from the presence of the LORD***.

The Bible says Yahweh gave Satan access to Job by saying all that Job has is in your power, or ***yad***, which speaks of the open hand. This is very interesting as we see the enemy functioning in a twisted measure of the hand. At this specific timeframe, the enemy was not allowed to physically lay his hand upon Job. One important factor in this entire narrative is the Lord could have chosen to address the satanic accusations by telling the enemy he had no access to Job at all. We know this is not the case, though. Yahweh knew His servant would be victorious. The thing is, I believe this encounter was in the heart and plan of God before the world began. God was not surprised by the enemy's visit and accusation. This was Job's path, the horizon for which he was ordained to walk. We must know with all confidence and certainty our Lord has the final say in all things, including removing the hedge if He chooses to do so.

How did Satan respond when given access to Job? The Scripture says he went forth from the presence of the Lord. All this discussion before Yahweh, angelic sons, and Satan just seems so strange and very bizarre. From our human perspective, we might think this should not have been permitted at all. Yet, it does happen, and we need to be very discerning as to what we can learn from all of it. Our enemy is spoken of as going forth from the presence, or face, of Yahweh. He goes forth to begin initiating his twisted plan, thinking in his corrupt mind that Job will turn his back on Yahweh.

How should a Job-like individual respond to Satan touching all that they have?

The above question is so hard to think about, especially in

terms of all the enemy could inflict upon him. I am in no way encouraging anyone to welcome such things to happen. However, we do need to remember the eternal mindset when we face these things or similar ones. God's motivation is for us to be victorious and overcomers. Our minds, will, and emotions can lead us into faulty thinking if they are not submitted to the perfect will of God.

> ***Job 1:20-22*** *²⁰ Then Job arose, and rent his mantle, and shaved his head, and fell down upon the ground, and worshipped, ²¹ And said, Naked came I out of my mother's womb, and naked shall I return thither: the **LORD gave**, and the **LORD hath taken away**; blessed be the name of the LORD. ²² In all this Job sinned not, nor charged **God [Elohim]** foolishly.*

Satan was allowed to touch everything Job had, including all his children and property. For the sake of time, I am not adding all the verses which speak of the destruction of his children and property, including all of his livestock (Job 1:13-19). This was such a devastating timeframe for Job, but I know from the first few verses of this chapter that, if Yahweh allowed this, according to His eternal plan, the servant of Yahweh would be triumphant in the end. Of course, we know the end of this narrative reveals this truth. Everything Job faced in the natural and spiritual realms were totally overseen by the eternal plan of Yahweh.

When faced with similar challenges, this must be our mindset. Submission, humility and worship are requirements as well. Job acknowledged that he came into the world with nothing. He knew and declared that Yahweh gives and Yahweh takes away, that, whatever took place in his life, he, determined in his thinking to bless the name of Yahweh. This is so important in the midst of opposition, to make declarations that are focused on blessing the name of the eternal plan rather than cursing it. In doing so, the Bible says Job did not sin, or miss the mark; nor did he charge Elohim, or the heart of God, in a foolish or frivolous way. We need to always remember this when we are facing warfare. Speak and release blessings, and do our best to not miss the mark or respond inappropriately to Elohim.[8]

At this point in all the difficulties Job had endured, he remained committed and immoveable in his devotion to the plan of Yahweh. Yet, Satan is allowed to come back on another day in the presence of Yahweh and the angelic sons of God. This time the tactic of the enemy was quite a bit different than before. Let's look at the scenario together.

> ***Job 2:1*** *[1] Again **there was a day** when the **sons of God** came to present themselves **before the LORD, [Yahweh]** and Satan came also among them to present himself **before the LORD. [Yahweh]***

Yahweh, Angelic Sons of God, and Satan at the Throne in Heaven

All of the individuals in these verses are spirit beings, and this is happening in the spirit realm. I am just reminding us of the spiritual setting, because this is something Satan and his forces are involved in on a day and night basis. Previously in this writing, I referenced how the enemy is focused on implementation and execution of his evil plan and agenda in the earth. The above verses give tremendous insight into the spirit realm and the inner workings and motivations of his evil heart. He wants to go after Job-like individuals attempting to influence the release of curses, not the blessings.

---

[8] Please obtain a copy of Walking with Elohim, by Ron Crawford from Pneumatikos Publishing at www.pneumatikos.com.

Another spiritual fact is all of this is transpiring in the spirit before the Throne of God in heaven. You might be thinking, how can this be since Lucifer was removed from heaven and fell as lightning. This is true, but according to the Scripture, the accuser of the brethren has not been completely removed from having access into heaven (Revelation 12:8). Of course, he does not have a permanent place, but access only, which is overseen by the Lord. At some point in the future, all access will be completely off limits; but until this happens, Job-like saints will be contested by the enemy.

Yahweh's Thoughts: Job Holds Fast His Integrity

This second account is very similar to the first in that Yahweh speaks of Job as a servant, none like him in the earth, a perfect and upright man, one who fears God.

> ***Job 2:2-3*** *2 And the **LORD [Yahweh] said unto Satan**, From whence comest thou? And **Satan answered the LORD, [Yahweh]and said**, From going to and fro in the earth, and from walking up and down in it. 3 And the **LORD [Yahweh] said unto Satan**, Hast thou considered my servant Job, that there is none like him in the earth, a perfect and an upright man, one that feareth God, and escheweth evil? and still he **holdeth fast his integrity**, although thou movedst me against him, to **destroy him without cause**.*

Yahweh begins the conversation with the enemy with these incredible descriptions of Job to Satan. I think this is great, because it reveals how Yahweh knows everything about those functioning in a Job-like walk before the Lord. These are dynamic qualities within the heart of an individual that Yahweh is fully aware of within His people. As I am studying and writing this, I am stunned by how the Spirit, or breath of God, is highlighting this in this hour. Think about all the calamity and difficulty Job encountered to this point, and what would be coming very soon. These are the thoughts Yahweh thinks towards those facing extreme demonically-driven situations manifesting in the spiritual and physical realms. He thinks these things during the good times, too. I am just focusing on the specifics of what is transpiring in the life of Job at this specific timeframe.

There is a thought from Yahweh in this instance that is not spoken in the first account. Nothing is outside the scope of the eyes of Yahweh, or His perfect vision. He has seen all the destruction upon his household and possessions. In this context, Yahweh declares to Satan Job still holds fast to his integrity. To me, this has powerful meaning as Yahweh is saying this about an individual upon the earth. To still hold fast speaks of being willing to stay the course and not give up no matter what is taking place. Job could have made the decision to not stay fastened to his calling and identity in God. Yet, he remained faithful and courageous in the midst of tremendous opposition. Yahweh spoke to his integrity, which speaks of his innocence. In other words, in the plan of Yahweh, Job had not done anything wrong.

Satan's Agenda: Destruction of Job Without Cause

The above statement is actually spoken forth by Yahweh to Satan. It does reveal some of the evil thoughts and intentions in the heart of Satan. Yahweh reveals things in the heart of the enemy by saying, you moved me to bring utter destruction to Job without cause. This was and still is part of the demonic agenda of Satan. Destruction without cause, or ***chinnam***, is the Hebrew word spoken of in this verse. In his book The

Fallen One,[9] Pastor Ron Crawford defines this term as a gift bereft of the qualifications of grace. This word was strategically employed by the enemy in his assessment of the relationship between God and Job. Essential to the enemy argument was an insight into the crucial nature of grace. According to Satan, the blessing of God was prominently upon Job, even though the man was without an investment of grace.

The enemy used this term to speak about Job fearing God, or Elohim for nought, or **chinnam** in Job 1:9. Yahweh reiterates this to Satan in his reference to the destruction of Job being identified without a cause, or **chinnam**, which stems from the root word for grace. The enemy was attempting to focus on a lack of grace in the life of Job. On the other hand, Yahweh was clearly focused on his devotion and faithfulness as a servant of the eternal plan. Satan thought he could see what appeared to be a lack of grace, which is an interesting twist, but we know the overcoming power of grace was known in the life of Job. We, too, are called to endure things like Job and stay the course so we can experience the elevating grace of God in our lives.

Satan Says

After Satan realized Job was not going to give in to his initial strategies of destroying his family and possessions, he speaks to Yahweh requesting access to bring severe infliction upon his physical body. His ultimate satanic objective was still destruction and cursing. The enemy is out to steal, kill and destroy.

Job 2:4-5 *[4] And **Satan answered the LORD**, [Yahweh] and said, Skin for skin, yea, all that a*

---

[9] Please obtain a copy of The Fallen One, by Ron Crawford from Pneumatikos Publishing at www.pneumatikos.com.

man hath will he give for his life. ⁵ But put forth thine hand now, and touch his bone and his flesh, and he will curse thee to thy face.

If you are like me, lots of questions come to mind. Why could Yahweh allow Satan to do these things to Job? Why would Yahweh allow for the destruction of his family? Why would Yahweh allow for the destruction of his possessions and livelihood? In the eternal plan of the Lord, He knows the end from the beginning and all the details in between. There was no way this would have been allowed to take place if Job would have turned his back on serving God. Even in all of these happenings, Yahweh dictated to the enemy what he could and could not do.

Yahweh Says: ...Save His Life

Job 2:6 *⁶ And the **LORD [Yahweh] said unto Satan**, Behold, he is in thine hand; but save his life.*

This is so important for us to remember in the midst of intense warfare. This kind of testing will come in different forms, but we need to recall God has not abandoned us just because things in the spirit and physical are challenging for us. Our mindset must be Yahweh's plan is still in action in our lives, and we need to not draw away from spending time in His Spirit, or His breath. This continual interaction will keep us in His perfect peace.

The ways of God are so different than the ways of man. When extreme circumstances of this nature occur, we must continue interceding in the spirit which will help ensure we continue our forward movement in the spirit and this world. Without this ongoing fellowship with His Spirit, we could be overcome rather than being overcomers. His eternal plan and mindset is for us is to step into being overcomers by His grace, which will always elevate individuals into new points of growth and development.

Satan Smites Job with Physical Challenges

At this point, the Bible says Satan went from the presence, or the face, of Yahweh and immediately began to continue his evil attacks by inflicting Job with severe physical challenges.

> ***Job 2:7-10*** *⁷ So went **Satan** forth from the presence of the LORD, and **smote Job with sore boils from the sole of his foot unto his crown**. 8 And he took him a potsherd to scrape himself withal; and he sat down among the ashes. 9 Then said his wife unto him, Dost thou still retain thine integrity? curse God, and die. 10 But he said unto her, Thou speakest as one of the foolish women speaketh. What? shall we receive good at the hand of God, and shall we not receive evil? **In all this did not Job sin with his lips**.*

-Physical Challenge: Smote Job with Sore Boils

I want to restate, Yahweh has specifically allowed Satan to test and inflict His servant with all of the challenges up to this point, including the physical ones mentioned above. I know this is difficult to grasp, but we must understand that once we have committed our lives into the plan of Yahweh, everything we experience in the spirit and physical realms are completely dictated and controlled by His eternal plan for us. The Hebrew word for smote in this verse is **naka**, which means to strike lightly or severely. In this case, Satan strikes a severe physical condition to Job in the form of sore boils. These kinds of boils are identified as burning, inflammatory ulcer-like manifestations on his physical body. This makes me cringe on the inside when I think about it. They covered his entire body from the sole of his feet to the crown of his head. I cannot fully comprehend this kind of physical challenge, but I am quite sure it was very painful, to say the least.

Job Speaks to Yahweh

Job did not really understand a lot of what was allowed to come against him from the beginning. Over time, as he committed to walk through all of the hardship and challenge, he gained incredible insights into the eternal plan and purpose of God. His experience in God should be a great point of encouragement to those functioning as sons and saints. The correct mindset is essential in the process and pathway of overcoming.

> ***Job 42:1***   *[1] Then Job answered the LORD, [Yahweh] and said,...*

Job's First Pronouncement to Yahweh: I Know You Can do Everything

When faced with very difficult testing and challenge, it can be very easy to not know or see the full picture of what our God is trying to do or accomplish. When this happens, as intercessors and saints, we must remain constant and confident in the eternal plan and purpose of Yahweh. As we commit to continue to stand, no matter how difficult it is in the natural realm, the time will come where the realization of what God is doing will be manifested and known in us. As Job is addressing Yahweh, he speaks some profound insights gained as he has walked through some rough waters. He declared to Yahweh he knows nothing is impossible with Him.

> ***Job 42:2*** *2 I know that thou canst do every thing,...*

It is very significant to take note of when Job feels led to speak, for the declaration about knowing Yahweh can do everything. He did not speak this forth before the challenges came his way. He made these powerful proclamations after walking through the hardships with Yahweh. It is in the midst of the times of testing we learn so much about who and what our God is fully capable of doing in our lives, even when we have no idea or cannot make sense of why things are happening.

Job's Second Pronouncement to Yahweh: No Thought Is Withheld from Thee

Another equally powerful pronouncement Job made to Yahweh was that no thought was withheld from Him. Job came to recognize and realize the all-knowing, perfect nature of Yahweh as he walked through the difficult circumstances with Him.

> ***Job 42:2*** *...and that no thought can be withholden from thee.*

Like Job, as we commit to developing and growing in our walk with Yahweh, we will come to realize insights experientially that are far more precious and meaningful than just head knowledge. For me, over the last year in facing challenging situations, I had a hard time grasping all that God was doing, but I knew He was with my family. At times, I felt like giving up and walking away, but chose to remain in walking with Yahweh's plan. I came to realize, with the help of the Spirit, no thought can be withholden from Him. This is a powerful phrase packed with insightful revelation regarding how the Lord knows everything.

The Hebrew word used for thought in this verse is ***mezimma***, which stems from the root ***zamam***, referring to Yahweh knowing all the plans, whether evil or good. As human beings, we lean on our own ability to understand sometimes, which can really cause us to not be in alignment with the eternal mind of God. When the Scripture says, no thought or plan, whether evil or good, is withholden from Him, we need to truly believe His Word. To be withholden means to clip off, to be isolated or inaccessible. All the plans are known and visible to the ears and eyes of Yahweh. There is not one thing isolated or inaccessible to Him. As partners and intercessors, we learn these powerful principles as we continue to walk and live in the Spirit. We are learning from Him in ways of His choosing. It is difficult during the process, but very rewarding in the end. Like Job, I have come to know Yahweh has complete control over all things happening in my life. He is really in absolute control.

Job's Third Pronouncement to Yahweh: I Have Uttered That I Understood Not...

Job makes another interesting pronouncement about himself in this scenario. He leads with a question followed by saying his utterances were made from his not understanding. We need to remember this as we walk through difficult situations or challenges.

> ***Job 42:3-5*** *3 Who is he that hideth counsel without knowledge? therefore have I **uttered that I understood not; things too wonderful for me, which I knew not**. 4 Hear, I beseech thee, and I will speak: I will demand of thee, and declare thou unto me. 5 I have heard of thee by the hearing of the ear: but now mine eye seeth thee.*

There are lots of lessons we can learn from what Job declares. One is we will not fully understand all that Yahweh is doing. We must trust Him and know He will be with us throughout everything we face in the spirit and in this life. Job spoke of these things as too wonderful for him, which he knew not. Yahweh is accomplishing so much in us, and they are too wonderful for us to fully know. We must remember this in the midst of our circumstances and quickly respond accordingly. We do not need to know all the details. Rather, we just need to trust and walk in patience, because whatever we face is filtered and overseen by the Almighty God.

Job's auditory and visual capacities came to know Yahweh in new ways. He speaks of this by saying I have heard of thee by the hearing of the ear, or auditory capacity, and his eye seeing Yahweh in new light. Experiences like these will cause our perceptive abilities to perceive in fresh ways. Job knew this to be a reality in his life, and I have come to know this realization in my life, too.

How did Job respond after making these profound pronouncements? The Bible says he abhorred himself, and entered into a time of repentance in dust and ashes.

> ***Job 42:6*** *6 Wherefore **I abhor myself**, and **repent** in dust and ashes.*

Job came to the realization that his actions and words throughout these difficult trials were not appropriate and, therefore, he needed to repent. This is exactly how he responded. As we walk through trying circumstances, we must always remember to come before God in repentance, if this is necessary for us. This will require some introspection , submission and humility on our part. As partners and intercessors, we will make mistakes along the pathway of purpose because we are flesh and blood. Do not enter into condemnation with this, though. If repentance is called for, submit, obey and move forward.

Yahweh Addresses the Three Friends

At this point in the life of Job, the Bible reveals some very important insights regarding the three friends. After Yahweh concluded speaking to Job, the Scripture says He specifically began a conversation with Eliphaz the Temanite. The communication was very direct and stern and speaks of His wrath being kindled against the three friends.

> ***Job 42:7-9*** *[7] And it was so, that after the **LORD** [Yahweh] had spoken these words unto Job, the **LORD** [Yahweh] said to Eliphaz the Temanite, My wrath is kindled against thee, and against thy two friends: for ye have not spoken of me the thing that is right, as my servant Job hath. 8 Therefore take unto you now seven bullocks and seven rams, and go to my servant Job, and offer up for yourselves a burnt offering; and my servant Job shall pray for you: for him will I accept: lest I deal with you after your folly, in that ye have not spoken of me the thing which is right, like my servant Job. 9 So Eliphaz the Temanite and Bildad the Shuhite and Zophar the Naamathite went, and did according as the **LORD** [Yahweh] commanded them: the **LORD** [Yahweh] also accepted Job.*

You might be asking, why was the wrath of Yahweh kindled towards the three friends? The main reason is because the three friends did not speak the thing that was right. Yahweh was not pleased with what these three individuals were speaking to Job, and He was letting them know and had specific requirements, such as offering seven bullocks and rams to the servant of Yahweh, Job.

Additionally, Yahweh stated His servant would pray for all of them, too. ***Palal*** prayer was offered by Job for the three friends instead of Yahweh dealing with their own folly, or foolishness, wickedness or crime. I am sure these three influences had good intentions, but they had no idea of what the Lord was saying or doing in the life of Job. They are spoken of as not declaring those things which were right. One major lesson that can be learned from this narrative: do not attempt to speak to anyone if you do not know what the Lord is really doing or saying. If we do like the three friends, we begin to proclaim words in a foolish manner. It is better to remain quiet in these cases than to speak forth words identified as being incorrect.

How did Eliphaz, Bildad, and Zophar respond to what Yahweh was requiring of them? The Scripture states they did according to what Yahweh was commanding of them. The directive of the Lord came forth, and these individuals had to make some choices. They could have easily decided to try and justify their words and actions. Yet, they knew obedience was necessary in making things right. What happened next in the life of Job was extraordinary!

Double Blessing and Provision

After all Job had faced in his life, it was time for radical change and provision from Yahweh. The Bible teaches the eternal plan of Yahweh turned the captivity of Job when he ***palal*** prayed for his friends and gave him twice as much blessing and provision than he had before.

> ***Job 42:10-15*** *[10] And the **LORD** [Yahweh] turned the captivity of Job, when he prayed for his friends: also the **LORD** [Yahweh] gave Job twice as much as he had before. 11 Then came there unto him all his brethren, and all his sisters, and all they that had been of his acquaintance before, and did eat bread with him in his house: and they bemoaned*

> *him, and comforted him over all the evil that the **LORD [Yahweh]** had brought upon him: every man also gave him a piece of money, and every one an earring of gold. 12 So the **LORD [Yahweh]** blessed the latter end of Job more than his beginning: for he had fourteen thousand sheep, and six thousand camels, and a thousand yoke of oxen, and a thousand she asses. 13 He had also seven sons and three daughters. 14 And he called the name of the first, Jemima; and the name of the second, Kezia; and the name of the third, Kerenhappuch. 15 And in all the land were no women found so fair as the daughters of Job: and their father gave them inheritance among their brethren.*

Provision and blessing were poured out in a double manner to Job. All his brethren, sisters and acquaintances came to eat bread with him in his house. They bemoaned and comforted him for all the evil that had been brought upon him. In addition, every man blessed him with a piece of money and earring of gold. Yahweh blessed the latter end of Job more than at the beginning. He had fourteen thousand sheep, six thousand camels, a thousand yoke of oxen and a thousand she asses and seven sons and three daughters. Job did not know this was going to happen until the time was right for it to manifest and come into fulfillment.

As saints and intercessors, we must never forget these powerful principles in the midst of harsh challenges and conditions. We are called to walk through the valley of the shadow of death, not to lay down and give up. We must know everything happens for a reason and is not outside of the scope and plan of Yahweh. As we commit to whatever the Lord is doing in our lives, whether we understand or not, we need to know provision and blessing will come at the exact time. Our mindset must be, nothing is beyond the oversight of the Throne of God. God has complete control over everything in our lives.

Lucifer

We have just seen how Satan was convinced he could bring utter destruction to Job by inflicting all kinds of evil upon him, resulting in him cursing the plan of God. Satan and all the forces of the dark realm are focused on killing, stealing and destroying.

Objective of Lucifer: Weaken the Nations

The enemy, or Lucifer, is also described as attempting to weaken the nations. Look with me in the Book of Isaiah, which reveals this tactic of the enemy.

> ***Isaiah 14:12-15*** *[12] How art thou fallen from heaven, O **Lucifer**, son of the morning! how art thou cut down to the ground, which didst **weaken the nations**! [13] For thou hast said in thine **heart**, [the heart of Lucifer] I will **ascend** into heaven, I will **exalt** my throne above the stars of God: I will **sit** also upon the mount of the congregation, in the sides of the north: [14] I will **ascend** above the heights of the clouds; I will be **like** the most High. [15] Yet thou shalt be brought down to hell, to the sides of the pit.*

The Luciferian nature wants to weaken, or overthrow or bring decay to nations. We are called to teach all nations according to the mandate of Jesus before His ascension to the Father. The two kingdoms are focused on the nations of the world, but with different motivations and objectives. The enemy in his fallen state cannot stand against the eternal plan and purpose of God. However, he will attempt to influence organizations and people to partner with his evil and corrupt plan and purpose.

The above verses reveal the evil heart of Lucifer. He clearly mentions a lot of his evil plans by saying the phrases, "I will ascend, I will exalt, I will sit, and I will be like the Most High." He could not stand that God would partner with mankind, and he determined to be a man-killer from the very beginning. His heart is bent on deception, decay and destruction, and he will not settle for anything less.[10] It is not my intention to focus on all of these descriptions, but rather to simply speak about the destructive nature of the enemy, and his evil agendas that are contrary to what God is wanting to accomplish on earth as it is in heaven.

In our previous section, Job initially had no idea of all the details of what was transpiring in the spirit realm. Satan was the instigator of all the evil unleashed against him. Yahweh allowed it because He knew Job would be victorious in the end.

Iniquity Being Found in the Anointed Cherub

Ezekiel also speaks about the enemy, describing him as the anointed cherub. He is depicted as being able to seal up the sum, full of wisdom, and perfect in beauty. His original place of operation was in Eden, the garden of God, and every precious stone was his covering.

> ***Ezekiel 28:11-19*** *[11] Moreover the word of the LORD came unto me, saying, [12] Son of man, take up a lamentation upon the king of Tyrus, and say unto him, Thus saith the Lord GOD; Thou sealest up the sum, full of wisdom, and **perfect in beauty**. [13] Thou*

---

[10] Please obtain a copy of The Fallen One, by Ron Crawford from Pneumatikos Publishing at www.pneumatikos.com.

hast been in Eden the garden of God; every precious stone was thy covering, the sardius, topaz, and the diamond, the beryl, the onyx, and the jasper, the sapphire, the emerald, and the carbuncle, and gold: the workmanship of thy tabrets and of thy pipes was prepared in thee in the day that thou wast **created**. [14] *Thou art the* **anointed cherub** *that covereth; and I have set thee so: thou wast upon the* **holy** *mountain of* **God**; *[Elohim] thou hast walked up and down in the midst of the* **stones of fire**. [15] *Thou wast* **perfect in thy ways** *from the day that thou wast created,* **till iniquity was found in thee**. [16] *By the multitude of thy merchandise they have filled the midst of thee with violence, and thou hast sinned: therefore* **I will cast thee as profane out of the mountain of God**: *[Elohim] and I will destroy thee, O covering cherub, from the midst of the* **stones of fire**. [17] *Thine heart was lifted up because of thy* **beauty**, *thou hast corrupted thy* **wisdom** *by reason of thy brightness:* **I will cast thee to the ground**, *I will lay thee before kings, that they may behold thee.* [18] *Thou hast defiled thy sanctuaries by the* **multitude of thine iniquities**, *by the* **iniquity of thy traffick**; *therefore* **will I bring forth a fire from the midst of thee, it shall devour thee**, *and* **I will bring thee to ashes** *upon the earth in the sight of all them that behold thee.* [19] *All they that know thee among the people shall be astonished at thee:* **thou shalt be a terror**, *and never shalt thou be any more.*

In his fallen state, Lucifer still has capabilities he operates in throughout the spirit realm. Of course, they have become corrupted since he decided to instigate the rebellion and convinced one-third of the angelic beings to partner with his evil agenda and plan. Ezekiel spoke of some powerful capacities and descriptions of the enemy. He is spoken of as the anointed cherub, being in the holy mountain of Elohim, which speaks of the heart of God. He was perfect, or complete in his ways from the day of his creation, and walked up and down in the midst of the stones of fire. At some point, his evil plan began to materialize and iniquity was found in him. As a result, he was cast as profane out of the mountain of Elohim or the heart of God.

Much more could be written about the enemy in this passage. My main point for referencing the enemy is to show some ways he functioned in his perfected state, but also how this led to his ultimate demise in being removed from heaven. He has an evil plan and intends to convince as many individuals to partner with it as possible. The enemy is focused on bringing deception into the world, attempting to even deceive the very elect. As the people of God, we do not need to glorify the enemy, but we also do not need to be ignorant of his devices.

2 Corinthians 2:11 *[11] Lest Satan should get an advantage of us: for we are not ignorant of his devices.*

Like Job, if Yahweh allows the enemy access to us, we must realize this is being allowed and not to bind and rebuke what the plan of God is allowing. It will be very tempting to engage in this way, but over time, the Spirit of God will make it very clear whether you should be binding and rebuking.

Angelic Releases of the Pure Fire from the Altar into the Earth

As we continue with the theme of fire in this writing, I was strongly directed to the following passage of Scripture, which speaks of a direct connection between the prayers of the saints and angelic releases into the earth. It is not my purpose to focus our attention on eschatological interpretations of when this will be taking place from pre-tribulation, mid-tribulation, or post-tribulation standpoint. There are a lot of timelines in the Bible we are just not going to really know from our own human perspective. I just know the Spirit of the Lord is highlighting this passage to me and revealing powerful insights regarding the timeframe in which we are currently.

> ***Revelation 8:1-4*** *[1] And when he had opened the seventh seal, there was silence in heaven about the space of half an hour. [2] And I saw the seven angels which stood before God; and to them were given seven trumpets. [3] And another **angel came and stood** at the altar, having a golden censer; and there was given unto him much incense, that he should offer it with the **prayers of all saints** upon the golden altar which was before the throne. [4] And the smoke of the incense, which came with the **prayers of the saints**, ascended up before God out of the angel's hand.*

It is important to remember John was still in the spirit as these things are were being revealed to him. I remember a specific day while in intercession and knew in this precise moment the passage was ignited in my mind and spirit. It speaks of the seven seals and seven angels which had seven trumpets. The Lamb was opening the seventh seal, or **sphragis**, which refers to a signet as fencing in or protecting from misappropriation. The stamp is impressed as a mark of privacy or genuineness. As this seal was opened, there was silence in heaven for about half an hour. After this occurred, an angel came forward and stood at the altar in heaven having a golden censer and was given much incense in which he should offer it with the prayers of the saints on the golden altar before the Throne of God.[11]

The angels are very much involved in the intercessory prayers being offered by the saints. God has designed this type of interaction and partnership, as angelic representatives have major roles in assisting, communicating and other various activities in conjunction with the saints. The visual picture of this passage clearly shows these things happening in heaven before the Throne. Not only are the angels drawn to intercessors and prayer, they are equally focused on affecting and being a part of the change God is releasing into the earth. After much incense is offered with the prayers of saints, the angel takes the censer and fills it with the pure fire from underneath the altar.

What is the main purpose of this fire? Where is God directing the angel to cast the fire? The main objective is for ignition and function within people in the earth. The Bible specifically says after the holy fire is gathered with the censer, the angel cast it, or ***ballo***, which means to throw in the earth.

> ***Revelation 8:5-6*** *[5] And the angel took the censer, and **filled it with fire of the altar**, [pure fire] and **cast [ballo – to throw]** it into the earth: and there were **voices**, [voices of intercessors calling upon God] and thunderings, and lightnings, and an **earthquake**. [6] And the seven angels which had the seven trumpets prepared themselves to sound.*

Within the spirit of every human being is the capacity to lift up their voice in intercession utilizing the gift of divers tongues, which is an amazing intercessory gifting to speak in the tongues of men and of angels. As the pure fire from

---

[11] Please obtain a copy of New Testament Grace, by Ron Crawford from Pneumatikos Publishing at www.pneumatikos.com.

heaven is released into the earth, a four-fold progression begins to happen with voices, thunderings, lightnings, and earthquakes. God looks for intercessors who will partner with Him in establishing His kingdom on earth as it is in heaven. Voices in this verse speaks of the activation of the hearts of individuals to begin calling upon God in intercession. God created His people to partner with Jesus who is continually making intercession for the saints to fulfill the will of God.

The fire from underneath the altar in heaven is being released into the earth by angelic representatives afresh in this timeframe. It is being directed to those who are hungering and thirsting after righteousness. God is releasing His pure fire to touch the spirits of His people that results in the voices of intercessors being raised up to partner with His eternal plan and purpose. God is looking for intercessors just like He was in the days of Isaiah.

In the next section, I want to focus on the reality of what it feels like to be in the perfect atmosphere in heaven. God is not affected by the things we are as human beings. We deal with all kinds of imperfections in and around us in this life. When we think about God and heaven, it must always be from a perfected state. God is perfect and all the various things in heaven are the same way. May God help align our thoughts and ways with His perfect ways.

Chapter 6

The Perfect Atmosphere in Heaven

The entire premise of the writing of this book stems from an encounter I was privileged to have with God in heaven before the Throne of God. After this initial experience, my spirit was carried away in the spirit on many different occasions into heaven where I was allowed to feel or sense the perfect atmosphere in this perfect place. Within the mind and heart of God, there is absolute perfection, unity and harmony. All of heaven functions in this same way. Let's begin by considering some verses and passages of Scripture which speak of the visionary capability of the Lord, or Yahweh, as it relates to His eternal plan and purpose.

Perfect Vision

The Perfect Vision of Yahweh: I Have Seen Your Affliction

Yahweh cares and sees what we, as individuals, are walking through in the spirit and in this life, too. We focus a lot on walking and living in the spirit, and we should, but we need to remember we are walking in the physical, too. We need to be spiritually minded, but this does not mean our body and soul are not involved in this process. As much as I would love to not be limited or affected by our sinful nature, we live in a flesh and blood body. I think our carnal, fallen nature speaks loudly at times about how God does not really see my situation or circumstance. We think these kinds of thoughts, yet Yahweh can see these kinds of things, too. Perfect visionary capability with no limitations at all. This is the God we partner with regarding His plan and purpose. It is an amazing reality when you think in this way…or better said, by thinking in His way.

> *Exodus 3:7*   *⁷ And the **LORD [Yahweh] said, I have surely seen [ra'ah]the affliction** of my people which are in Egypt, and have heard their cry by reason of their taskmasters; for I know their sorrows;*

The Vision of Yahweh: Looks/Ra'ah at the Heart

Before we begin, I want to ask you a series of questions to consider in light of the above reality. How does Yahweh see? What is He looking at in an individual? Church? Nation? What is He looking at when His eyes scan throughout the world? What did the Lord see in the heart of David that moved Him to choose him as the next king? What was it that caused Him to say this is the next king? Yahweh is always looking into the depth of the heart, which is the opposite of the way man looks.

Samuel Looked Initially the Way Man Looks

Just a word of caution. Samuel the prophet, whose words did not fall to ground, assessed in this manner. We need to take notice and be extremely cautious in the way we function in our discernment. We are not ever going to perfectly assess situations or circumstances correctly all the time, but we need to know Yahweh will speak during these times to help and assist us when we are not looking through the eyes of Yahweh. This is not a word of rebuke in any way, just a reminder for all us of the eternal importance of our carnal inclinations that must be continually submitted to the directives of the eternal plan of God.

Yahweh Ra'ah/Sees the Heart vs. Man Looks at Outward Appearance

He does not look on things that mankind deems important or noteworthy. His vision is perfect and He is not really focused on the physical characteristics of individuals. He is not necessarily looking at age, gender, ethnicity and the like. He is looking at the central place of the heart of an individual. Yahweh has the capacity to see things in the hearts of children, youth, men and women that we cannot see unless He reveals it to us by His Spirit.

1 Samuel 16:1-10   *¹ And the **LORD said** unto Samuel, How long wilt thou mourn for Saul, seeing I have rejected him from reigning over Israel? fill thine horn with oil, and go, I will send thee to Jesse the Bethlehemite: for I have provided me a king among his sons. ² And Samuel said, How can I go? if Saul hear it, he will kill me. And the **LORD said**, Take an heifer with thee, and say, I am come to sacrifice to the LORD. ³ And call Jesse to the sacrifice, and I will shew thee what thou shalt do: and thou shalt anoint unto me him whom I name unto thee. ⁴ And Samuel did that which the **LORD spake**, and came to Bethlehem. And the elders of the town trembled at his coming, and said, Comest thou peaceably? ⁵ And he said, Peaceably: I am come to sacrifice unto the LORD: sanctify yourselves, and come with me to the sacrifice. And he sanctified Jesse and his sons, and called them to the sacrifice. ⁶ And it came to pass, when they were come, that he **looked** on Eliab, and said, Surely the **LORD'S anointed** is before him. ⁷ But the **LORD said** unto Samuel, **Look not on his countenance**, or on **the height of his statur**e; because I have refused* *him: for the LORD seeth not as man seeth; for man looketh on the outward appearance, but the **LORD looketh on the heart**. ⁸ Then Jesse called Abinadab, and made him pass before Samuel. And he said, Neither hath the LORD chosen this. ⁹ Then Jesse made Shammah to pass by. And he said, Neither hath the LORD chosen this. ¹⁰ Again, Jesse made seven of his sons to pass before Samuel. And Samuel said unto Jesse, The LORD hath not chosen these.*

Yahweh's vision is focused on what is inside the heart of humans. He does not see like us. I am astounded by the revelation of these things as I type them. I have known these verses and passages, but the Father is peeling away another layer in a line upon line way. Life in the spirit is completely different than the life we live in this physical realm.

Yahweh's Anointed

1 Samuel 16:11-13 *¹¹ And Samuel said unto Jesse, Are here all thy children? And he said, There remaineth yet the youngest, and, behold, he keepeth the sheep. And Samuel said unto Jesse, Send and fetch him: for we will not sit down till he come hither. ¹² And he sent, and brought him in. Now he was ruddy, and withal of a beautiful countenance, and goodly to look to. And the **LORD said**, Arise, anoint him: for this is he. ¹³ Then Samuel took the horn of oil, and anointed him in the midst of his brethren: and the **Spirit of the LORD** came upon David from that day forward. So Samuel rose up, and went to Ramah.*

God chose for David to be the next king. Samuel almost made a terrible mistake in trying to determine who would be functioning as Yahweh's anointed. As a people we cannot, nor should we, use physical appearances to determine the chosen of the Lord. Yahweh brought a corrective word to the prophet initially;, and when the right individual was in front of him, the Lord directed Samuel to arise and anoint. This was to be done in the presence of his brethren. From that point forward, the Spirit of the Lord, or Yahweh, was upon David. The ***ruwach*** of Yahweh, or the breath of the eternal plan and purpose came upon, which is the word ***salah***, and it means to push forward. This is what happens in the spirit when the Spirit of the Lord comes upon a person.

This is so interesting, because there are different dimensions of the breath of God referenced in the Scripture. This aspect is known as the Spirit of the Lord, which speaks of the eternal plan and purpose of God. This dynamic release upon an individual is very important, as it focuses on someone stepping into new dimensions of experiencing and knowing the plan and purpose of Yahweh. This specific aspect of the breath of God will always cause an individual to be moved upon and pushed forward in the things related to the eternal plan and purpose.

M'nuwchah Rest, Eternal Plan and Vision of Yahweh

I was led to the following passage below one morning while studying and doing my due diligence to seek for understanding of what God has been doing in my heart. I am so overwhelmed by what He is speaking freshly about one of the ways Yahweh's vision functions, or at for whom He looks. His vision is perfect in every way, not being confined, restrained or obstructed by anyone or anything.

Isaiah 66:1-2 *¹ Thus saith the **LORD**, [Yahweh] The heaven is my throne, and the earth is my footstool: where is the house that ye build unto me? and where is the place of my **rest**? [m'nuwchah] 2*

> *For all those things hath mine hand made, and all those things have been,* **saith [an oracle, from na'am - to whisper, to utter as an oracle] the LORD**: *[Yahweh] but to* **this man will I look, [nabat - to scan, to look at intently with pleasure, favor, or care]** *even to him that is* **poor** *and of a* **contrite spirit**, *[ruwach] and* **trembleth at my word**.

Heaven and earth are spoken of in the above verses. The eyes of my heart were opened to an entirely new revelation concerning the vision of Yahweh, or one of the ways He sees. I was privileged to be taken in the spirit with the Lord to experience these verses this morning. I was so overwhelmed during this time as my spirit was interceding in new ways and sensing His eyes being upon me. It is such a sobering and humbling encounter. I felt His Spirit, or breath, in such an amazing way and knew with complete certainty He is fully aware of all things. God knows exactly what we need at the exact time. I say this because before any of this insight and experience took place, I was wondering if God really knows what we face in this life. We are human and still must deal with our carnal nature, so this was one of the moments I was thinking about if God truly knew what my family was going through at this time. Better yet, did God really know personally what I was facing at this time.

Little did I know a visitation of His Spirit would soon be happening. I was not prepared for what was about to take place. I just knew in my mind I was thinking about our current situation and circumstances. We need to be a people who are living in the Spirit, or breath of God. This goes way beyond just quoting
Scripture or memorization. It is experiential and exploratory as His Spirit leads and directs us in our spirit.

So, what does it mean for the plan of Yahweh to look? The Hebrew for look is **nabat**, and it has incredible meaning of the inner workings regarding the plan of God. It means to scan, to look at intently with pleasure, favor or care. As I was reading the above verses, I could feel my a stirring in my spirit and knew the significance of these words were being given to me at this specific time. As the intensity of the stirring increased in my spirit, I laid myself down on floor in **proskuneo**, ,and His Spirit began impacting me in such a deep way as I continued to pray in the tongues of men and of angels. I just partnered with Him for a while on this spiritual journey. I became very much aware that the plan of God is at work on our behalf, even when we feel otherwise.

What is Yahweh looking for in an individual? His visionary capability is focused on finding various individuals who are poor and contrite in spirit, or **ruwach**, or the place of His dwelling and trembling at His word. Yahweh is scanning the globe and looking for certain things in the **ruwach** within individuals. We focus too much on the things of the earth. Let's look at some specific things Yahweh looks towards in the hidden place of mankind.

What makes this such an amazing revelation is manifold, but one worth mentioning revolves around how to catch the eyes of Yahweh. To illustrate this, I want you to think with me for a moment of what it feels like when someone you care for in a deep manner notices something special about you. It feels very good. It could pertain to any kind of physical appearance of beauty or a new hairstyle. My point is, as human beings we notice and look upon the physical appearance and can sometimes unknowingly not recognize a lot of the inner qualities of human beings. Yahweh does not look on outward appearance, but on the heart of an individual. It does not mean he cannot see all the physical qualities or characteristics; it just means the very person of who He is focuses on the hidden places within mankind.

Poor and Contrite in *Ruwach*

First, the individual that catches the vision of Yahweh is someone who is identified as being poor in spirit or ***ruwach***. I had not noticed before in these verses how the words poor and contrite are within the spirit of the individual. The word for spirit is the term used to describe the breath of God. In this context it speaks of how Yahweh can identify someone who truly recognizes their need for something, and contrite in the place where His eye is looking, which is in the ***ruwach*** of the person. Jesus spoke of being poor in spirit, or ***pneuma***, in the New Testament, too.

> ***Matthew 5:3*** *³ Blessed are the **poor in spirit***: *for theirs is the kingdom of heaven.*

To be poor and contrite comes from the Hebrew words ***anah*** and ***nakeh***. ***Anah*** speaks of a need, or an individual being in a situation or condition that is not very good. In fact, if you look at the term, it refers to being depressed in our environment or in the mind. ***Nakeh*** actually refers to being smitten and can refer to being maimed or dejected in some instances. This seems puzzling to me because being poor and of a contrite spirit sounds like these are good things in God, and they really are necessary in our walk. To be in this depressed state speaks of our need and reliance upon Yahweh no matter what we are facing in our circumstances or in our thought processes. We must know His plan is at work even when we think the struggles are outside the scope of His vision. We need to continually remind ourselves this is not the case.

I must be honest with you. The idea of being contrite in spirit is difficult for me to understand. By definition, it means to be smitten, maimed or dejected. No matter what we are facing in this life, we need to remember His eternal plan can transform our minds to feel and experience His breath, resulting in a dynamic change in our circumstances and minds. The breath of God comes with great intent and purpose, and the very essence of His Spirit is full of words and insights regarding your eternal plan and purpose. The Spirit has been gently probing me in my thinking to really meditate on what happens when the breath of God is released into our minds and spirits. He is not in the business of wasting His breath when He communes with us in our spirits, or the place of His rest. When He opens our perceptions to know and feel His Spirit, we need to know contained in His breath are words of His plan and purpose for us. May God help us in learning to live in His breath, as it is the most satisfying and fulfilling relationship in heaven and on earth.

Trembles at the Word of Yahweh

Yahweh also looks at an individual who trembles at His word. To tremble means to have a reverential fear for the word regarding Yahweh's eternal plan and purpose. The Hebrew word is **hared**, which comes from the root **harad**, meaning to shudder with terror, fear or hasten. As I was reading this, I remember having a visitation in the spirit where my entire being -- soul, body, and spirit -- was trembling before the Throne while I was in intercession. I shuddered for quite some time as this manifested in my entire being. I was sensing this coursing from the tips of my toes to the top of my head.

Let me ask you a question. If you did not have any human being ever look upon you, how would this make you feel? Would you feel shunned, ashamed, angry, rejected, sorrowful? I am sure you would feel some of these things and much more. Who would you rather have look upon you, a human being or Yahweh? I can assure you, as important as it is for a human being to look upon you or me, there is no comparison with, the Lord, or Yahweh looking upon us. It was during an intercessory encounter that I felt the gaze of Yahweh looking upon the depth of my spirit that I experienced a greater measure of this reality. It was breathtaking and left me speechless. I could feel His eternal pleasure, favor and care as this was happening.

No Sleep nor Slumber in Yahweh

As I continue to describe the perfect atmosphere of heaven, it stands to reason to speak of how Yahweh never slumbers nor sleeps. Rest in heaven is not needed and does not take place. Energy and resources are limitless.

> ***Psalm 121:1-8*** *¹ I will lift up mine eyes unto the hills, from whence cometh my help. 2 My help cometh from the LORD, which made heaven and earth. 3 He will not suffer thy foot to be moved: he that keepeth thee **will not slumber**. 4 Behold, he that keepeth Israel shall neither **slumber** nor **sleep**. 5 The LORD is thy keeper: the LORD is thy shade upon thy right hand. 6 The sun shall not smite thee by day, nor the moon by night. 7 The LORD shall preserve thee from all evil: he shall preserve thy soul. 8 The LORD shall preserve thy going out and thy coming in from this time forth, and even for evermore.*

In some ways, it is kind of challenging to think of not needing any rest, because as human beings we need rest to be replenished to continue being productive from day to day. Some individuals require seven to eight hours of sleep a night, while others can continue to function with much less. The perfect atmosphere in heaven continues to fully function without the need to rest at all.

In the above passage, Yahweh's plan is spoken of as being our help. As we lift our eyes to the hills, we come to realize our help has nothing to do with anything in this world. Rather, it comes from knowing and functioning in the plan and purpose of Yahweh. He will not suffer our feet to be moved, and He is able to keep us because He will not slumber nor sleep. I cannot fully comprehend such incredible realities. Yet, I know enough in my mind and spirit that Yahweh is fully capable of helping and preserving His people and is not affected by drowsiness or sleep. Heaven never rests and is continuously working towards the saints fulfilling the will of God.

No Rest in Heaven

Another powerful reality about the perfect atmosphere of heaven involves all the spiritual beings in this perfect place. This passage of Scripture is speaking of locale as being before the Throne in heaven.

> ***Revelation 4:5-11*** *⁵ And out of the throne proceeded lightnings and thunderings and voices: and there were seven lamps of fire burning before the throne, which are the seven Spirits of God. ⁶ And before the throne there was a sea of glass like unto crystal: and in the midst of the throne, and round about the throne, were four beasts full of eyes before and behind. ⁷ And the first beast was like a lion, and the second beast like a calf, and the third beast had a face as a man, and the fourth beast was like a flying eagle. 8 And the four beasts had each of them six wings about him; and they were full of eyes within: and **they rest not day and night**, saying, Holy, holy, holy, Lord God Almighty, which was, and is, and is to come. 9 And when those beasts give glory and honour and thanks to him that sat on the throne, who liveth for ever and ever, 10 The four and twenty elders fall down before him that sat on the throne, and worship him that liveth*

for ever and ever, and cast their crowns before the throne, saying, 11 Thou art worthy, O Lord, to receive glory and honour and power: for thou hast created all things, and for thy pleasure they are and were created.

The four beasts are spoken of as not resting day or night while declaring the holy purpose of God. I believe it is safe to declare all of heaven…,which includes the Father, Son, Holy Spirit, Four Beasts/Cherubim, Seraphims, Gabriel, Michael and his angels, angels of God/Elohim, angels of the Lord/Yahweh, innumerable angelic representatives, heavenly hosts and all the various operations of heaven do not need rest. They function day and night in complete perfection and harmony with nothing wavering. This is remarkable to consider and equally mind-boggling to encounter in the spirit realm.

I remember on several occasions being carried away in the spirit into heaven. While in this perfect place, my mind and spirit could see and perceive the perfect atmosphere. As I was interceding in heaven, I remember every part of my being was affected by the absolute perfection to the degree I could not put into words its impact on me. I just remember being completely transformed in my thinking and felt a lasting heavenly imprint in my mind and spirit. It was a life-changing experience; I hope this eternal imprint will forever be a part of my existence and will not fade away.

No Tears, Death, Sorrow, Crying or Pain in Heaven

Heaven is a place where there are no tears, death, sorrow, crying or pain. John writes about this in the Book of Revelation 21. He speaks of God making all things new. This is a reference to the perfect nature of heaven, and we can experience this now, not just in the future.

> ***Revelation 21:3-4*** *[3] And I heard a great voice out of heaven saying, Behold, the tabernacle of God is with men, and he will dwell with them, and they shall be his people, and God himself shall be with them, and be their God. [4] And God shall wipe away all **tears** from their eyes; and there shall be no more **death**, neither **sorrow**, nor **crying**, neither shall there be any more **pain**: for the former things are passed away.*

As saints and intercessors, when we are granted access to function in these heavenly ways, our minds and spirits will be forever impacted by the eternal atmosphere of heaven. It is not affected by any negativity or anything that we allow to influence us as humans. The cares of this world can and easily distract and influence what we do in this life. God and all His heavenly hosts are tireless in their pursuits in establishing the will of God on earth as it is in heaven.

As I have been privileged to be taken in the spirit into various heavenly places, God and all the heavenly hosts function with exact precision and perfection. They are flawless in their endeavors, which includes the partnership being offered to mankind. As I have thought more about this reality, I felt directed to put together a list of various things that do not take place in heaven versus some of the things that do take place. Below is a sampling and is in no way a comprehensive list.

- No Forgetfulness
- No Unrighteousness
- No Stress
- No Corruption
- No Slumber

- No Sleep
- No Division
- No Uncleanness
- No Doubt
- No Unbelief
- No Iniquity
- Perfect Unity and Harmony
- No Hopelessness
- No Ungodly Fear
- No Lack of Courage
- No Death
- No Sorrow
- No Crying
- No Pain
- No Distrust
- Faith
- Hope
- Love/Agape
- Righteousness
- Mercy
- Grace
- Eternal Life
- Perfect Satisfaction
- Perfect Fulfillment
- Perfect Peace

The desire of God is for us is to experience Him in His fullness now, not just when we go to heaven. The concept of going to heaven should be a present tense reality in the lives of every born-again Christian. Sadly, this is just not the case for some believers. God has so much in store for His people, if we would just be willing to trust Him and make ourselves vulnerable to the moving of His Spirit within and around us. It is never the intention of God for any human being to seek fulfillment and satisfaction apart from Him. Every human was originally created in pure perfection to commune with God like Adam and Eve in the ***ruwach*** of the day. This was the target of the serpent in the garden of Eden. He wanted to sever the relationship mankind had with God, and initially succeeded in a convincing fashion.

Through the blood of Jesus Christ, the invitation to commune and fellowship with God in spirit has been completely restored. We have the opportunity to have deep, ongoing relationship with our Father by His Spirit to the place within every born-again spirit. It is spirit to spirit commune. Our spirit man has the capacity with no limitations to move in the spirit, which means it can function in heaven and in other heavenly places in many ways. Individuals such as Ezekiel, John and Paul were caught up and carried way into the spirit realm and encountered heavenly things that are beyond this world.

As I am writing this, my heart is remembering back on the times my spirit was carried into heaven. While in heaven and other heavenly places, I was so consumed by the atmosphere and always remember it being absolutely without any imperfections. I could literally feel this in my mind and spirit as I was engaged in what was transpiring within and around me. I cannot promise that you will experience these kinds of encounters or visitations, as they are at the discretion of the Father, but I can guarantee your spirit was created in the image of the heart of God and you can commune with and know Him intimately. Our Father wants to commune with us, His Spirit to our spirit. Deep relationship is what is the most important thing in this life. Nothing of this world can bring true satisfaction and fulfillment like our heavenly Father. He created us to know Him and function in our identity, and the pathway to know this is through ongoing relationship.

With this in mind, our spirit has the capacity to move and

function in the spirit realm in many ways. Intercessory prayer is so important in knowing God and His ways. He is looking for individuals that will partner with Him in intercession at the right hand of God in heaven. The intercessory gift that transformed my relationship and prayer life is the grace gift of divers tongues. The revelation of this amazing gift was revealed to my pastor and dear friend, Ron Crawford. If you would like to learn more about this necessary gift, you can obtain a copy of this from Pneumatikos Publishing.[12]

Casting All Your Care Upon Him

As human beings, it is so hard for us to not get caught up or entangled with the things of this life. We face various kinds of challenges from day to day, including all sorts of distractions. Peter writes about our need to continually remain humble and to cast all of our care upon God because He really does care for us.

> *1 Peter 5:6-7* *⁶ Humble yourselves therefore under the mighty hand of God, that he may exalt you in due time: ⁷ Casting all your **care** upon him; for he careth for you.*

Humility is always going to be a necessary in moving forward in God. Humility leads to God exalting us in His time. As this occurs, we also have a responsibility to cast all our cares, which are references to distractions, upon God. Casting literally means to throw upon. So, what are we to throw upon God, anyway? The Scripture is very clear:, it is all of our cares, which really is speaking of anything that would be a distraction. According to the dictionary definition, this would refer to

---

[12] Please obtain a copy of Divers Tongues, by Ron Crawford from Pneumatikos Publishing at www.pneumatikos.com.

anything that is attempting to divide our attention, or prevent concentration. A self-examination is essential in determining what attempts to derail us in our walk with God.

What is trying to divide your attention? Or, what is trying to prevent you from concentrating on the things of the Spirit? We cannot make it in this life if we do not release the distractions to God. I believe this is done as we come before our God in relationship and continue to pray in the spirit. As this happens, the Spirit, or breath of God, can consume our minds and spirits causing all the distractions of the world to fall by the wayside. Any time you feel like the cares of this world are trying to overtake you, get in the spirit realm and allow the Spirit of God to fill your mind and spirit. I can promise you, this works every time without fail.

Notice how we are instructed to cast ALL our distractions, not just a few or some. All means exactly what is says. Anything that brings distractions, attempting to keep us from pursuing the things of the Spirit, needs to be willingly given to God. Why? Because the Bible says He cares for us. To care in this verse comes from the Greek word ***melo***, which means to be of interest to, or to concern. Our God is very interested and concerned with what we are experiencing in this life and knows all kinds of distractions cannot and must not be carried by us. I can promise you, God knows everything that comes against you, or in this case, distracts you, from His eternal plan and purpose. Humble yourself and surrender all of the cares of this world to Him. You will feel so much better as you relinquish these things to the Lord.

As the title of this book indicates, God passionately desires to be an all-consuming fire within each of us. There are so many different things in this life trying to consume our thinking and way of living. As previously mentioned in this writing, there is not anything in this life that brings true satisfaction and fulfillment. Relationship and functioning in our spiritual identity is the pathway that leads to life, satisfaction, and fulfillment. I have come to this realization in the last few months in ways that left me completely stunned in my mind and spirit. Perfect passion and love reside within the heart of God. [13]

> *1 John 4:18* *[18] There is no fear in love; but **perfect love [agape]** casteth out fear: because fear hath torment. He that feareth is not made perfect in love.*

It is through a passionate relationship with His perfect **agape** that will cast out every measure of fear. His Spirit can extinguish anything that is not from Him. Fear is associated with torment, which can paralyze our passionate pursuit. Pursue Him and partner with His Spirit, because this is what we were created to do in this life. Do not allow anything to prevent this from happening. The enemy will try to stop or prevent this kind of **agape**-driven pursuit, but always remember to make this relationship your main priority.

Fire does many things in the scripture. It is my prayer God will cause your spirit to be engaged in His passionate fire within His heart, which will cause you to be completely consumed with His desires and intents and not your own. When this happens in spirit, you will forever be changed by Him. You will begin to know the reality of the greatest thing given to you is His perfect love, or **agape**.

> *1 Corinthians 13:13* *[13] And now abideth faith, hope, **charity, [agape]** these three; but the greatest of these is **charity.** [agape]*

1 Corinthians 13 is a relationship passage that has been

---

[13] Please obtain a copy of Agape, by Ron Crawford from Pneumatikos Publishing at www.pneumatikos.com.

misused in a lot of ways. It speaks of various characteristics of what the perfect *agape* love of our Father is and is not. It is time for Christians and churches across the world to have a divine experience with the love of God that flows forth from His heart. God never intended for these expressions to merely be spoken forth at weddings and funerals. If read in its proper context, these words are never really used in this chapter. *Agape* is something that is so real, and God wants us to know this reality in our day-to-day commune with Him.

May God help us and continue to take us deeper into His mind and heart as He is moving His church forward in a rapid fashion. You can be a part, but it will require dying to self so you can know what He desires and wants for His church. May our Father put His passion in our minds and spirits to breathe hard after His eternal plan and purpose. We are created to function and be consumed by His holy fire.